AMERICAN THEATRE
BOOK OF MONOLOGUES
FOR WOMEN

AMERICAN THEATRE
BOOK OF MONOLOGUES
FOR WOMEN

EDITED BY STEPHANIE COEN

THEATRE COMMUNICATIONS GROUP
NEW YORK
2003

Introduction, "Be Specific: The Actor's Approach to the Monologue" (An Interview), and monologue introductions copyright © 2003 by Stephanie Coen

American Theatre Book of Monologues for Women is published by Theatre Communications Group, Inc., 520 Eighth Ave., 24th Floor, New York, NY 10018-4156

This publication is made possible in part with funds from the New York State Council on the Arts, a State Agency.

TCG books are exclusively distributed to the book trade by Consortium Book Sales and Distribution.

LIBRARY OF CONGRESS CATALOGING-IN-PUBLICATION DATA

American theatre book of monologues for women / edited by Stephanie Coen.—1st ed.
p. cm.
Audition monologues selected from plays first published in American theatre magazine since 1985.
ISBN-13: 978-1-55936-198-9
ISBN-10: 1-55936-198-0 (pbk. : alk. paper)
1. Monologues. 2. Acting—Auditions. 3. American drama—20th century.
4. Women—Drama. I. Coen, Stephanie. II. American theatre magazine.

PN2080.A48 2001
812'.045089287—dc21   2001027314

Cover design by Carin Goldberg
Book design and composition by Lisa Govan

First Edition, August 2003
Third Printing, January 2009

ACKNOWLEDGMENTS

I am grateful to Todd London, editor of TCG's previous volumes of *Contemporary American Monologues*, in whose footsteps I have happily followed for many years. I owe a great deal to TCG's exemplary publications department, particularly Terry Nemeth for the opportunity, Kathy Sova for her judicious editing, and Todd Miller and Gretchen Van Lente for their able assistance.

Thanks also to my bosses, present and past: Bartlett Sher, artistic director of Intiman Theatre; Jim O'Quinn, editor of *American Theatre* magazine; and the three leaders of the field whom I was lucky enough to work for during my seven years at TCG: Ben Cameron, Lindy Zesch and, especially, Peter Zeisler, who taught me more than he might know, and whose lessons I still value.

I owe a special debt to all of the playwrights whose work is included in this volume for their talent and generosity, and for allowing us to include excerpts from their plays, in some instances cobbled together to make sense out of context. Where lines of dialogue or stage directions have been cut, a bracketed ellipsis [...] marks the deletion. There were instances when we were asked to retain all characters and their dialogue within a scene; we have done so, setting the connective material within brackets and indenting it.

For my parents,
and for Yohanan, Avigail
and Elinoam Ben-Gad

CONTENTS

INTRODUCTION

In the November 1985 issue of *American Theatre*, critic James Leverett introduced the first play published in the magazine, Emily Mann's *Execution of Justice*, with these words: "This month *American Theatre* begins what we all hope will be a long, distinguished career of play publication with a work that is not supposed to exist: a play by a contemporary American author concerning events and issues of historical scope and import."

Very nearly two decades and (as of July 2003) 100 scripts later, *American Theatre*'s record of play publication is, indeed, long and distinguished. The monologues included in this volume were all culled from texts that were published, often for the first time and always in their entirety, in the magazine. Whether or not all of these plays reflect "historical scope and import" is, of course, a matter of debate. What remains indisputable is that they are, together, a record of the contemporary American theatre, of what our playwrights were thinking and writing about as the millennium approached (to borrow a phrase) and the new century began.

From the first issue, the magazine's mandate was, in part, to select plays that had already been produced in a number of theatres. There was no directive to "discover"—or hype—the latest talent. By seeking out new plays that were being produced throughout the country, however, the magazine helped bring adventurous, provocative and original writers to greater public attention and critical acclaim, often with their earliest works. Before the first decade passed, *American Theatre* had published Eric Bogosian, Constance Congdon, Christopher Durang, Maria Irene Fornes, Craig Lucas and George C. Wolfe, to name only a half-dozen of an impressive assemblage. In later years, Edward Albee, Steven Dietz, Tony Kushner, Donald Margulies, Suzan-Lori Parks, Sam Shepard, Octavio Solis, Paula Vogel, Naomi Wallace—and so many others—would join them.

These writers and the others published by *American Theatre* (and in Theatre Communications Group's book program) are of different generations and disparate backgrounds, with shared influences but idiosyncratic styles and sensibilities. Their plays take many forms and are many things—wild riffs on history, absurdist comedies and dramatic reveries, elegies for loss, explorations of the families we are born into (usually dysfunctional) and the families we create, and fierce mediations on what it has meant to be "other" in America. They range from the personal to the political to the poetic (although some are both political and poetic simultaneously), with excursions into farce, autobiography and, of course, the well-made play.

The structure of this book is borrowed from TCG's previously published volumes of monologues, *Contemporary American Monologues for Men* and *Contemporary American Monologues for Women*, both of which were edited by the astute and inimitable Todd London. As in the earlier collections, the monologues are grouped in named chapters by themes and connections, rather than broken down according to the actor's age range or the style of the work. Relevant information about the character and other necessary background about the play is included in the introductory paragraph to each piece. A glance at the chapter headings should give you a quick sense of the emotional tenor or subject matter of the works that will follow.

For the actor, the intention of this volume is to provide strong material for use in auditions or acting classes. As excerpted, the monologues are meant to be resonant pieces independent of their original dramatic context, but I encourage you, more than anything else, to read the plays from which they are extracted—the best and truest way to uncover their full potential and understand your character. (Publication information is included at the back of this book, in the Further Reading section.)

As a collection, these plays are a testament to TCG, and *American Theatre*'s, commitment to the enduring ambitions of contemporary playwriting. "Make sure if you're trying to impress me with the depth and complexity of your work that you've got material to match it," director Bartlett Sher says in the interview that follows. "If you want your work to be rich and interesting, the monologue needs to be rich and interesting." These selections reflect some of the best and most surprising voices in the contemporary theatre. Now it is for you, as an actor, to bring these pieces to life, and by so doing, fully explore and inhabit the worlds that they evoke.

—S.C.

BE SPECIFIC: THE ACTOR'S APPROACH TO THE MONOLOGUE

**An Interview with Bartlett Sher,
Artistic Director, Intiman Theatre, Seattle**

What should an actor look for in choosing audition material?
I always answer this question based on my own instinct, not from what's going to get an actor a job. Never pick something you wrote. It's a terrible idea, not because you might not be a good writer, but because I can't evaluate it honestly. I want you to be there to act, and interpret something you didn't write.

It's important to pick something that is right for you, in the obvious sense that it would be a part you would be good at playing. If you have played a part—and played it well, and were really guided in it—I would use it. That's more important than showing versatility. The monologue should also be close to the part for which you're auditioning. Many things are being evaluated: speech and voice work, to some extent physical skills, and being able to play through a clear single action in the course of the monologue.

If I'm auditioning for a Shakespeare play, even a small part, and all I have is the monologue to go on, I want to see that the person is so good at the monologue, so close to the character, that I might find them useful for other parts in the play. If I'm auditioning for *Richard II*, I'm not going to cast

Richard out of a general monologue audition, but I might learn that I could find a Bushy, a Bagot or a Green. You need to pick a monologue that shows how good an artist you are *and* how valuable you will be in the other parts. I've often become interested in people who are great with verse, who are funny, who are pure and clear and still and strong.

What makes a good audition monologue?

It's important that you are playing a single action, and that I watch you playing an action. Actors will often try to illustrate everything that is going on in the whole play—so I never see the actual acting, I see all the results. They will do, for instance, Edmund's speech from *King Lear* about being a bastard, and they will show what a terribly bad person they are. But that speech is also about Edmund coming to a conclusion and working his way through a problem. All Shakespeare monologues come in three parts—a beginning, middle and an end—and the revelation of the speeches is always about what the character is trying to do or work out.

Actors need to get the focus on what their character is trying to accomplish, instead of on the character itself. People tend to do monologues alone and take out the other characters in the scene. But even if it's a Shakespeare soliloquy and you are alone, there is always interaction. Always be very specific about who the audience is to the character at that moment—are they a best friend, are they a confidant, etc. When they are not just "the audience," you can play the action and be in the scene more completely. Otherwise you may just be performing, as opposed to acting.

What about working with a monologue from the contemporary theatre?

It's always appropriate to stay within the genre you're working. If you are auditioning for a comedy, make the monologue a comedy; if it's a tragedy, make it a tragedy. In a general audition, your common sense will tell you what you're good at. I always like simplicity and purity, as opposed to using the monologue to "feel" something. That's always the worst. If somebody comes in and they're crying by the end of the monologue, that's a nightmare.

Actors should approach contemporary writers with the same level of care and scoring and attention to language and rhythm that they do Shakespeare. If it's David Mamet or John Guare or Arthur Miller or Harold Pinter, there's usually an internal rhythm, and a real choice of language, that reveals potent and profound information over the course of the monologue. Often people will get relaxed in the language and become more concerned about the "performance"; yet the language has all the real information in it.

When an actor walks into an audition, what are you looking for?
I usually audition intensively—like a diagnostic test. I will take the actor through a series of choices and see what they can pull off. I won't necessarily have in my head a set thing. Obviously, there are things that the part requires, and there are things that the person brings to the part, in terms of intelligence and heart. Those are the two critical things—mind and heart.

If the audition is conducted without a monologue, and it usually is, I'm testing for whether or not I'm going to have a good collaborator. So I will ask questions to see what kind of responses I get, to gauge the actor's level of thinking. If it's an audition with a monologue, what usually happens is that people try to use the monologue to show *all* the things they can do well. They will illustrate every line, emotionally, physically or verbally. They will pack it with all the things that they are good at. So now it's not an experience of a monologue in time, it's an experience of a résumé in the form of a monologue. But it's more important that an actor make one choice (or a few strong choices) and hold with that, rather than make too many choices.

How does it affect you, as the caster/director, if you know the work, and you are aware of the context of the monologue within the play?

That's hard, because you get into a region where my supposedly intelligent opinion intersects with your choices. What hopefully *won't* happen is that I think I'm so smart that I'm just going to tell you how to do it. If you did the monologue really well and I thought you were really on it and it looked like you could do it—that is, be in the play, in that part—I will have discovered that you have some chops. I won't learn anything if you are using it to do anything else, like break down and cry.

What are the pitfalls of an audition—what should an actor avoid?

As I said, anything you wrote yourself. Anything personal—don't believe *in* anything, play a character. People often turn monologues into testimonies; acting is not about telling me something you feel about the world. Otherwise it's *Oprah*. I need to see characters that don't know what they believe in because they're in the middle of it.

Don't pick material that's too mundane, because sometimes your work will be better than the material. And you can never beat the material—the material will always win. So make sure if you're trying to impress me with the depth and complexity of your work that you've got material to match it. If you want your work to be rich and interesting, the monologue needs to be rich and interesting.

Anything narrative is really bad—if it's narrative, you're not playing anything, you're telling me a story. The character has got to be somebody in the middle of circumstances, playing an action on somebody else. If there is a clear facility for language, if you are clearly playing to or against another person, if your work is clearly fresh and on the thoughts, I am going to listen better. If I'm seeing you be a character in specific circumstances, then I'm wondering what's going to happen by the end of the monologue. That's all a monologue has to do.

Let's talk about humor in an audition—how hard is it to be funny?

It's not that hard—if you are a funny person. It's not easy to do in the case of creating funny voices and goofy walks. That's a different kind of funny. Usually humor is about being deep in the circumstances, and about reaching some level of pain, panic and agony, which leads to those circumstances getting out of control. If it's really active, then it's funny. When it isn't active, then it isn't funny.

We all have seen a lot of date plays, love plays, relation-ships plays—and usually it's the pain of failure that makes the joke. Irony and sarcasm are really hard to pull off, because they are a little bit too smart.

What about an actor's physicality?

I'm exceptionally attuned to physicality, to relaxation and a quiet body, as opposed to a frenzied one. If a physical choice is made, it's got to be extremely precise. I have no set rules, like more physical or less physical; you just have to be very good at whatever you choose to do, and very clear and specific. As an audition goes on I'll bust anybody whose body is not behaving, or is not really connected. In the silhouette of a character, in the physical signature of a character, is an enor-mous amount of information. If somebody makes a strong physical choice, and they pull it off, it can be extremely reveal-ing and extremely impressive.

How do you work with the actor in the audition?

If an actor has laid down a good path in a monologue, I'll then give them choices to play with to see if I can push them some-where, and that then becomes a small model of what rehearsal will be like—are they versatile, do they get the idea, do they understand what I'm talking about, do they have the chops to implement something? I'll take them through a lot of colors, line to line to line to line, to see if they have versatility and to keep them on track of the action. It's at this time that I start to find out if somebody has a propensity for working with me or not.

They don't have to do what I'm looking for, but they have to do something interesting that's going to take the material somewhere new that neither of us might have expected. That's when you begin to see a possible collaborator—they listen really well; they respond in an interesting and creative way; they take the work somewhere that is either exactly what I had in mind and reveals it fully, or somewhere completely different that amazes us both. I don't like people who enter the profession because they were talented and have a series of tricks at their disposal. That's not as interesting to me as having real collaborators who have their own ideas.

Are the rules different when you're working with a student in a classroom situation?
The rules are never different. There may be different levels of skill, but the rules of what it takes to make the work good are never different. What makes a person rich and interesting in their work is probably not known, even to that person. It's just a lot of practice and a lot of talent—and talent is the most mysterious thing. What is one person's talent versus another's is unknown, but it's either there or not there. It either plays loud and big in them or it is small and tiny, and you can't tell why.

Do actors have "types"?
I prefer to cast against type, but sometimes type is type. I've worked in a lot of companies where we frequently had to cast against type, and it would almost always have good results, especially in a play that people knew; it subverted the audiences' expectations and allowed the play to be something fresh. But there are certain types that must be obeyed, and therefore you really have to get somebody who is right inside of that. Not every person in a show can be cast against type.

Actors hate type because it makes them feel that they are categorized, and I don't blame them. It's the hardest thing in the world to find two great ingénues, because all actors want to be character actors: they all want to be something else. Getting somebody who is really good at being an ingénue—surprising and rich and attractive and fun—is harder than finding a good character actor.

What would your advice be when an actor comes in for an audition—play to type or against it?

It depends on what they want. If they are good at their type, know they're good at their type and want to tell me that they're good at their type, that's what they should do. If they have versatility, or if they believe they can really nail an ingénue and also play one of the clowns, they should do both.

If you know yourself, and are connected to what you can do well, then you should show me. If you don't know yourself and are not connected, you're going to try to show me something that you don't really feel close to, and I'm not going to get it. Or, if I do, it will be a false representation of who you are anyway. Some people are great rock stars and bad actors. Some great actors can convince me they're rock stars. As an actor, it's the hardest thing in the world to learn who you are, and accept who you are, and then be able to play with and mold that. There are different kinds of actors; the ones who do one kind of thing really well, and those who do many things well.

How might these personal qualities that you're talking about manifest themselves in an audition?

Some people tend to believe that their personality will be so fun and engaging that no one will be able to resist their charm when it comes to the audition. Often it is the reverse: it can make me really annoyed, because I like the personality to be displayed in the work.

Lots of actors get taught to be very obedient, and that's not it either. If you get asked a lot of questions, don't just slavishly obey and try to make the person who is holding the audition happy. Actors are always afraid they are going to be rejected—that's all over them—they torture themselves, and then there's too much neediness in the interaction that leads to the audition. Be yourself, and be professional. Put your work out there and then let it go. You might be right for the part, you might not.

One last question—do you have a favorite monologue?

I don't, but I have some that I've heard an awful lot. In the Shakespeare world, there's a couple that you hear all the time. I've been in the middle of productions where I've thought, This would make such a great monologue, how come I've never heard it? Usually it's because the monologue only has a single thought in it, and people then don't do it. There's Posthumus' monologue in *Cymbeline*, for instance, where he rails against women. It's a hateful, evil monologue that's just as interesting as Edmund's bastard speech in *King Lear*, which I've heard one billion times. I always like to be surprised, and I like to be reassured.

"Surprised and reassured"—what do you mean by that?

If somebody's doing two monologues, you want to know that they are really good at what they do, and then you want to be surprised. Sometimes both happen at the same time, but not always. Monologue auditioning is difficult because it's sort of lateral to what the work is going to be—it's only a way of introducing yourself, not a way of finally getting the part. As a way of introducing yourself, it's best to choose a monologue that reflects what's extremely wonderful about you.

Bartlett Sher is artistic director of Intiman Theatre in Seattle, Washington, where his credits include the commissioned world premiere of *Nickel and Dimed*, a play written by Joan Holden and based on the book by Barbara Ehrenreich, which debuted as part of Intiman's thirtieth anniversary season in 2002. He made his Seattle directing debut in 2001 with Shakespeare's *Cymbeline* and directed a new production of the play for Theatre for a New Audience, which premiered in England at the Royal Shakespeare Company with an American cast, and had an award-winning Off-Broadway run in New York. For the New York production, he received the 2002 Joe A. Callaway Award from the Stage Directors and Choreographers Foundation. His additional credits include Molière's *Don Juan* and the American premiere of Harley Granville Barker's 1907 play *Waste* (2000 OBIE Award for Best Play), both produced by Theatre for a New Audience. Prior to coming to Intiman in 2000, he served as associate artistic director at Hartford Stage Company, company director at the Guthrie Theater and associate artist at the Idaho Shakespeare Festival. He has taught and run workshops throughout his career in the United States and internationally.

1

"WAS I WRONG TO SIDE WITH THE LIVING?"

MARISOL

By José Rivera

At the dawn of the millennium, New York is an apocalyptic battleground. The moon has not been seen in nearly nine months; apples are extinct and food turns to salt; derelict men give birth to stillborn babies. Marisol's Guardian Angel is decked out for guerilla warfare; she is "a young black woman in ripped jeans, sneakers and black T-shirt. Crude silver wings hang limply from the back of the Angel's diamond-studded leather jacket." While Marisol is sleeping, the Angel describes all the times she has saved Marisol's life—and explains that she must leave her to lead an insurrection against God.

ANGEL: I kick-started your heart, Marisol. I wired your nervous system. I pushed your fetal blood in the right direction and turned the foam in your infant lungs to oxygen. When you were six and your parents were fighting, I helped you pretend you were underwater: that you were a cold-blooded fish, in the bottom of the black ocean, far away and safe. When racist motherfuckers ran you out of school at ten, screaming . . . [. . .] . . . I turned the monsters into little columns of salt! At last count, one plane crash, one collapsed elevator, one massacre at the hands of a right-wing fanatic with an Uzi, and sixty-six thousand six hundred and three separate sexual assaults never happened because of me. [. . .] *(The Angel is nervous now, full of hostile energy; anxious)* Now the bad news. [. . .]

I can't expect you to understand the political ins and outs of what's going on. But you have eyes. You asked me questions about children and water and war and the moon: the same questions I've been asking myself for a thousand years. [. . .]

The universal body is sick, Marisol. Constellations are wasting away, the nauseous stars are full of blisters and sores, the infected earth is running a temperature, and everywhere the universal mind is wracked with amnesia, boredom and neurotic obsessions. [. . .] Because God is old and dying and taking the rest of us with Him. And for too long, much too long, I've been looking the other way. Trying to stop the massive hemorrhage with my little hands. With my prayers. Believing if I could only love God more, things would get better. But it didn't work and I knew if I didn't do something soon, it would be too late. [. . .] I called a meeting. And I urged the Heavenly Hierarchies—the Seraphim, Cherubim, Thrones, Dominions, Principalities, Powers, Virtues, Archangels and Angels—to vote to stop the Universal ruin . . . by slaughtering our senile God. And they did. Listen well, Marisol: Angels are going to kill the King of Heaven and restore the vitality of the universe with His blood. And I'm going to lead them.

A QUESTION OF MERCY

By David Rabe

Inspired by Dr. Richard Selzer's New York Times Magazine *essay about his personal experience with the issue of assisted suicide, David Rabe's play explores what happens when Anthony, stricken with AIDS, decides to end his life and the effect of that decision on his survivors—his lover Thomas and their dearest friend Susanah. Immediately before this speech, delivered to the audience, Susanah has "fired" Anthony's doc-*

tor—who had agreed to assist Anthony's suicide—after convincing Thomas that they will all be caught by the police.

SUSANAH: My philosophy—if I can call it that—has always been more about the interpersonal moment. In other words, what are we doing? What can we do? These two men were my friends. Anthony was the dear one. I mean, the one who was a delight. He was fun and startling, the way he would come up with the precisely appropriate gesture that was somehow totally unexpected. But Thomas moved me more. And that's why I ended up doing what I did. At least, I think it is. There was Thomas and he was going to live after all this, wasn't he? Did the extremity of Anthony's circumstances eliminate every other concern? Was I wrong to side with the living? I know there are counterarguments, but in the version of the dispute I conducted within myself the conclusion seemed absolute. I had to protect Thomas. For the longest time, I didn't know what I was to do, and I had the wisdom and patience not to act— not to be rash, but to wait until it came to me, until I knew the function I was to provide. And once I knew, I did it. It's my strength, really. It's my virtue. Anthony needed a protection I couldn't grant. But what Thomas needed was within my reach. So I gave it.

MISS EVERS' BOYS

By David Feldshuh

Miss Evers' Boys *is based on a true event in American history— the now infamous Tuskegee Study conducted in Alabama in the 1930s, in which nearly four hundred African-American men were secretly denied treatment for syphilis and deliberately lied to by public health officials. Miss Evers, nurse to a group of these poor sharecroppers, was convinced to partici-*

*pate in the study against her better judgment. In this mono-
logue, the final speech of the play, she testifies four decades
later during a 1972 Senate subcommittee investigation into
human experimentation.*

MISS EVERS: In the testimony today, there was a man gra-
cious enough to wonder what effect the scandal, as he put it,
might have on the public health nurse who has worked with
participants and who lived in Tuskegee. "She has been known
throughout the program as a selfless woman," he said, "who
devoted her entire career to this project." And then he was
kind enough to hope that it would "not be necessary for her
to share any of the blame." Well, now there's big blame and
then there's little blame. The big blame—that seems to be
going to the government and those doctors. Some people in
Macon are even saying the government gave those men that
disease in the first place. I don't know. I don't know about
that. I only know about the little blames. It's the little blames
that I'll have to be handling. Those are the blames that got
nothing to do with talk about right and wrong and black and
white and guinea pigs and money. Those little blames are
when you go back to where you live, lived for your whole life,
and catch your friends looking at you for no seeming reason,
and people walk by you and don't say "good morning" and
they don't use your name when they're giving you change as if
using it would dirty their mouths up some. Newspapers don't
publish stories about these little blames but they mount up
and they're strong and they push you to live a new way of life.
(Strong, not apologetic or self-pitying) I loved those men.
Those men were susceptible to kindness.

THE DARKER FACE OF THE EARTH

By Rita Dove

In her first full-length play, former U.S. Poet Laureate Rita
Dove recasts the Oedipus story on an antebellum plantation
in South Carolina. Phebe is a slave in her early teens with an
"electric" presence. She was raised in Massa Jennings's "big
house," where her mother took care of his privileged daugh-
ter, Miss Amalia. Phebe tells the story of her mother's death to
Augustus Newcastle, a new arrival to the plantation who rouses
his fellow slaves with talk of revolution.

PHEBE: Mama worked in the kitchen until
 I was about five; that's when
 fever broke out in the quarters.
 She used to set table scraps out
 for the field hands, and I
 stuck wildflowers in the baskets
 to pretty 'em up. Mama said
 you never know what a flower can mean
 to somebody in misery.
 That fever tore through the cabins like wildfire.
 Massa Jennings said the field hands
 spread contamination and forbid them
 to come near to the house, but
 Mama couldn't stand watching them
 just wasting away—so she started
 sneaking food to the quarters at night.
 Then the fever caught her, too.
 She couldn't hide it long.
 And Massa Jennings found out.
 (Gulps a deep breath for strength, reliving the scene)
 Mama started wailing right there at the stove.
 Hadn't she been a good servant?

Who stayed up three nights straight
to keep Massa's baby girl among the living
when her own mother done left this world?
Who did he call when the fire
needed lighting? Who mended the pinafores
Miss Amalia was forever snagging on bushes?
Mama dropped to her knees
and stretched her arms along the floor.
She didn't have nowheres to go;
she'd always been at the Big House.
"Where am I gonna lay
my poor sick head?" she asked.
He stood there, staring
like she was a rut in the road
and he was trying to figure out
how to get around it.
Then he straightened his waistcoat
and said: "You have put me and my child
in the path of mortal danger,
and you dare ask me what to do
with your nappy black head?"
He didn't even look at her—
just spoke off into the air
like she was already a ghost.
(Woodenly:)
She died soon after.

2
"I HAVE TO DO PENANCE."

ABINGDON SQUARE

By Maria Irene Fornes

Marion is "preciously beautiful, modest [and] obedient." She marries her husband Juster—a man thirty-five years her senior—when she is fifteen and recently orphaned, at a time when "she needed a mother more than a husband." All of that, however, is soon to change. Maria Irene Fornes's play explores Marion's sexual awakening and its consequences for her marriage over the course of nearly a decade (1908 to 1917). In this speech, set three years after the start of her marriage, she describes the furtive, sexually charged encounters she has with the anonymous man who has become her obsession (and, later, will become her lover).

MARION: It was he. There was no doubt in my mind. I saw him and I knew it was he. [. . .] I hid behind the stacks. [. . .] I took a book and buried my head in it. I was afraid. I thought if he saw me he would know and I would die. He didn't. I saw him leave. For a moment I was relieved he hadn't seen me and I stayed behind the stacks. But then I was afraid I'd lose him. I went to the front and I watched him walk away through the glass windows. Then, I followed him . . . a while . . . but then I lost him because I didn't want to get too near him. I went back there each day. To the bookstore and to the place where I had lost him. A few days later I saw him again and I followed him. Each time I saw him I followed him. I stood in corners and in doorways until I saw him pass. Then I followed him.

I was cautious but he became aware of me. One day he turned a corner and I hurried behind him. He was there, around the corner, waiting for me. I screamed and he laughed. He grabbed me by the arm. And I ran. I ran desperately. I saw an open entranceway to a basement and I ran in. I hid there till it was dark. Not till then did I dare come out. When I saw that he wasn't there I came home. I haven't been outside since then. I'll never go out again, not even to the corner. I don't want to see him. I don't want him to see me. I'm ashamed of myself. I'm a worthless person. I don't know how I could have done what I did. I have to do penance.

AN AMERICAN DAUGHTER

By Wendy Wasserstein

Judith B. Kaufman is a highly regarded specialist in oncology or, as she mockingly calls herself, "a nice Jewish African-American doctor." "Boisterous and energetic," Judith is a career woman in Washington, D.C., where for some time, and at much expense, she has been trying without success to get pregnant. "I love Judith, and Judith was the character who really connected with audiences, too—which is odd, because Judith is one angry girl!" Wendy Wasserstein commented in an American Theatre *interview. "Judith is alone, and I find that profoundly moving." Here, she tells her best and oldest friend, Lyssa, that she tried to drown herself.*

> *Note: the "festival of regrets" is a Jewish tradition in which breadcrumbs, symbolizing repentance, are tossed into water during the High Holy Days.*

JUDITH: I went to the festival of regrets. I prayed by the banks of the Potomac. There were old men davening in prayer shawls, and young lawyers in Brooks Brothers suits. I watched while the men tossed in their breadcrumbs of secret sorrow. "Oh Lord, my god, I cheated on my income tax. Oh Lord King of the universe I lust for the Asian check-out girl at Hany Farms delicatessen. Oh Lord, I have sinned, I dreamt about a strip of bacon." At first I remained silent. I stood there feeling my familiar distance and disdain. And then, almost involuntarily, I began shredding my low-fat cranberry-orange muffin. I wanted this God, this Yahveh, to know me. So I tossed my first crumb into the water. "Oh Lord, my God, King of the universe, I have failed to honor my mother and father," and that regret floats out to Maryland. "Oh Lord, my God, I distrust most people I know, I feel no comfort in their happiness, no sympathy for their sorrow." A tiny cranberry sits still upon the water. "Oh Lord, our God, who is like you in earth or in heaven, I regret the men I've been with, I regret the marriage I made, I regret never having children, I regret never having learned to be a woman." I pull off the entire top and a wad of muffin sails like a frigate towards the Washington Monument. "Oh Lord, my God, Mighty of Mighty, Holy of Holy, I can't make life and I can't stop death. Oh Lord, my God, the Lord is one, I've wasted my life," and I jump in. [. . .]

It seems I'm still a very good swimmer. [. . .] The Potomac isn't very cold in September. It's still warm from the summer night. [. . .] I was great. I was bobbing up and down in my pearls and Liz Claiborne suit, when I noticed a box of Dunkin' Donut holes floating along. And suddenly I remembered the slogan from my mother's favorite donut shop, "As you ramble through life, brother, whatever be your goal, keep your eye upon the donut, and not upon the hole." And I began laughing and laughing. Now I had a purpose. Now I had a goal. I must rescue the donut holes and bring them here to you on N Street. Lyssa, these are the donut holes of my discontent!

THE GIMMICK

By Dael Orlandersmith

The Gimmick *is a full-length monologue about a young girl growing up in Harlem with dreams of becoming a writer, her friend Jimmy who dreams of becoming an artist, and the divergent paths that befall them when Jimmy falls victim to drug addiction. Near the end of the play, Alexis, feeling betrayed by Jimmy and in enormous pain, allows Jimmy's addict father "Darkman Clarence" to do the "in + out, in + out . . . there's blood / blood / blood / Lost-My-Cherry Blood."*

Note: Lenny is Alexis's alcoholic mother; Ms. Innis is the librarian who introduces Alexis to James Baldwin, Tolstoy, Kafka and the power of words.

ALEXIS: I'm in my room cutting up clothes / clothes I had on when Clarence took me / bloody clothes / I cut up bloody clothes / ripping them with my teeth / with the scissors.

I bring them to my neck / want to slice myself / waste myself / slice myself / I close my eyes / Jimmy's in the foreground / Scissors / I trace my neck / face / with the scissors / The kill yourself / kill myself voices / they're in my head / loud / clear / Kill yourself / kill myself voices / I can hear them loud / Jimmy's in the foreground / In my head with the voices / gonna waste himself / gonna waste myself / erase myself / I look into the mirror / I see flesh / fat, burdensome flesh / I see waste / waste / I trace the scissors over my body / it's waste / I want to end it / Life / life's a Gimmick / The voices are loud / strong / Somewhere I hear Lenny's voice / "Why can't you be thin?" / Pretty / thin / pretty / The kill yourself / kill myself voices / all the voices / they separate / collide / separate / collide / Jimmy's in the foreground / I can see him nodding / nodding / opiate mumble nods / I trace the scissors / over my body / it's waste / I want to end it / life's a Gimmick / The voices are loud / I see the empty space / the space where my portrait was / where myself was / I gave him myself in the portrait / he took it / now I'm looking at the wall where it was / the space / empty.

The voices grow louder / there is no God / I'm still holding onto the scissors / want to slash myself with the scissors / Lenny / she said Jimmy's nothing / I got dropped by a nothing / I'm nothing too / Waste / waste / I'm waste / The scissors / I aim for my gut / trace my gut with the scissors.

I spot Jimmy / Jimmy Baldwin / I see his book / his words near the pile of clothes / How'd that book get near the clothes? / I pick up the book / [. . .] Ms. Innis somewhere / somewhere says, "Don't waste" / And the other Jimmy / Jimmy Baldwin smiling / smiling to me / big grin / laughing eyes / smiling to me / he's smiling to me.

Ms. Innis / James Baldwin / are louder than Lenny's words / louder than the kill yourself / kill myself voices / "Words / use words" / I reach for my pen / I reach for language / for the words in me / Those words will make me beautiful, strong / will make Jimmy beautiful, strong / will create beauty / My words / My stroke of words / I will make them / From Harlem I will make them carry me from Harlem to Paris / from ghettos to palaces / My words / my vision / and Jimmy's in the background / I'm in the foreground / I'm in the foreground / Paris on my fingertips / glittering on my fingertips.

3

"MY BABIES!"

THE MARRIAGE OF BETTE AND BOO

By Christopher Durang

The marriage of Bette (nee Betsy) Brennan and Boo Hudlocke is not destined for happiness. Bette has one healthy baby, then gives birth to four stillborn children; Boo drinks. From an early scene in this dark comedy, with Bette still in her wedding dress, she "talks cheerfully and quickly, making no visible connections between her statements," speaking directly to the audience.
    Note: Emily is Bette's other sister.

BETTE: First I was a tomboy. I used to climb trees and beat up my brother, Tom. Then I used to try to break my sister Joanie's voice box because she likes to sing. She always scratched me though, so instead I tried to play Emily's cello. Except I don't have a lot of musical talent, but I'm very popular. And I know more about the cello than people who don't know anything. I don't like the cello, it's too much work and besides, keeping my legs open that way made me feel funny. I asked Emily if it made her feel funny and she didn't know what I meant; and then when I told her she cried for two whole hours and then went to confession twice, just in case the priest didn't understand her the first time. Dopey Emily. She means well. *(Calls offstage)* Booey! I'm pregnant! *(To audience)* Actually I couldn't be, because I'm a virgin. A married man tried to have an affair with me, but he was married so it would have been pointless. I didn't know he was married until two months ago. Then I met Booey, sort of on the rebound. He seems fine though. *(Calls out)* Booey! *(To audience)* I went to confession about the cello practicing, but I don't think the priest heard me. He didn't say anything. He didn't even give me a penance. I wonder if nobody was in there. But as long as your conscience is all right, then so is your soul. *(Calls, giddy, happy)* Booey, come on!

THE MARRIAGE OF BETTE AND BOO

By Christopher Durang

After delivering her second stillborn child, Bette calls Bonnie Wilson, her best friend when she was a child. Together they were "the two stupidest in the class." "Bonnie," their teacher used to say, "your grade is eight, and Betsy, your grade is five." This is one of the memories Bette conjures to reintroduce herself to her old friend, with whom she has not spoken in many years.

BETTE: Hello, Bonnie? This is Betsy. Betsy. *(To remind her)* Bonnie, your grade is eight, and Betsy, your grade is five. Yes, it's me. How are you? Oh, I'm sorry, I woke you? Well, what time is it? Oh I'm sorry, but isn't Florida in a different time zone than we are? Oh. I thought it was. Oh well.

Bonnie, are you married? How many children do you have? Two. That's nice. Are you going to have any more? Oh, I think you should. Yes, I'm married. To Boo. I wrote you. Oh, I never wrote you? How many years since we've spoken? Since we were fifteen. Well, I'm not a very good correspondent. Oh, dear, you're yawning, I guess it's too late to have called. Bonnie, do you remember the beach and little Jimmy Winkler? I used to dress him up as a lampshade, it was so cute. Oh. Well, do you remember when Miss Willis had me stand in the corner, and you stand in the wastebasket, and then your grandmother came to class that day? I thought you'd remember that. Oh, you want to go back to sleep?

Oh, I'm sorry. Bonnie, before you hang up, I've lost two babies. No, I don't mean misplaced, stupid, they died. I go through the whole nine-month period of carrying them, and then when it's over, they just take them away. I don't even see the bodies. Hello? Oh, I thought you weren't there. I'm sorry, I didn't realize it was so late. I thought Florida was Central Time or something. Yes, I got twelve in geography or something, you remember? Betsy, your grade is twelve and Bonnie, your grade is . . . what did you get in geography? Well, it's not important anyway. What? No, Boo's not home. Well, sometimes he just goes to a bar and then he doesn't come home until the bar closes, and some of them don't close at all and so he gets confused what time it is. Does your husband drink? Oh, that's good. What's his name? Scooter? Like bicycle? I like the name Scooter. I love cute things. Do you remember Jackie Cooper in *Skippy* and his best friend Sukey? I cried and cried. Hello, are you still there? I'm sorry, I guess I better let you go back to sleep. Good-bye, Bonnie, it was good to hear your voice.

TONGUE OF A BIRD

By Ellen McLaughlin

Dessa is a single mother. Her daughter Charlotte, who is twelve, was abducted while hiking with the Girl Scouts. When the play begins, Charlotte has been missing for eleven days. Desperate, Dessa hires Maxine, a search-and-rescue pilot, to search for her daughter. This first speech is from Dessa's initial meeting with Maxine, just after she has offered her as payment an antique watch.

DESSA: That's what I got. Heirloom. I got no more money. I spent it on posters and stuff, this asshole detective, Carl What's-his-face, the milk cartons— [. . .] —But I figure it's a plane that's going to—'cause if you could just see her—And the money's just—'cause I don't have time to waste, she's—I've been emptying out my . . . So you can have the, this, there's still some money, I've just got to get it out of the bank, just . . . I got your name and called you and I came here right away so I just picked up the watch . . . *it doesn't matt*er . . . I'm sitting in that fucking house all day, all night, I'm looking at all this shit, these *things*, and you can have anything, come over, take a look, in fact, do me a favor, rent a U-Haul, like a huge one, pull it up outside the door and just start loading it up, couch, TV, oven mitts, shampoo bottles, bath mats, clocks, celery sticks, just take it—and then get some suction thing, some supersonic vacuum thing, park the hose at the front door and get the, the, everything, the air, the dust on the walls, between the cracks, the sounds left over in there, and, while you're at it, *me*—yeah, suck me right up out of that place and then the house itself after me, like in some cartoon, if you can do that, porch, banister, walls and windows, get it all, don't leave any-thing, just a hole, just nothing, not even a hole, nothing, and drive away. If you can find her, if that would help find her, 'cause I'm telling you, whatever it takes, I don't give a shit any-more. I just want her back. I just want my daughter back.

TONGUE OF A BIRD

By Ellen McLaughlin

Dessa describes her reaction upon being told by the police that children almost always know the person who abducted them, and reveals parts of her life to Maxine for the first time.

DESSA: They told me all that. First thing. *Very* interested that I don't know exactly who her father is. My whole, like, com-pletely fucked-up personal life just lying on the police linoleum there like puke. They couldn't really get it, that I'd just run like hell, put this huge distance between me and anybody who could have been her father. Out of maybe six guys. Just came up here. Put my finger on the map. I thought, OK where in the world is it, like, completely nowhere and nobody knows me. OK Loon Lake, that sounds nice. I thought, she'll like that, the baby. Loons. And around it, green map color. Nothing much. Trees. There was that little picture of the tree on the map. Pine trees. And none of these guys will ever know, not that they would care much. I'm not going to flatter myself here, but they wouldn't be able to find me even if they wanted to. And no one ever knew I was pregnant. That I know. Nobody from my life before. [. . .]

She doesn't look like anyone I've ever known. She's completely different. And whoever took her, whoever that was, she'd never seen him before. I know that. Whoever the fuck that was.

The night after the polygraph test I fell asleep in the, the police station there. I put my head down on the desk and bam, like I'd been slugged on the head. Had the print of somebody's paper clip on my cheek for like two days. But here's the thing. What I dreamt was that I *did* abduct her like they said. I'm telling you, oh God, what an incredible relief. I'd just *forgotten* that I did. And I'm standing at the sink, doing dishes and I'm looking out the window at this little green garden shed out back, it's like falling over, about the size of an outhouse, tiny, you know, and I'm looking at it and I suddenly remember that Charlotte, I put her out there *myself*, in the shed, it was all so, like, well, *of course*, how stupid of me, causing all of this trouble, I just forgot. I don't think I've ever been so happy. It all, finally, made perfect sense.

BURIED CHILD

By Sam Shepard

This Pulitzer Prize–winning play is a gothic, dysfunctional-family comic tragedy. Halie, the matriarch, describes her three sons: Bradley, an amputee; Tilden, who is "profoundly burned-out and displaced"; and Ansel, the dead hero. For most of the first scene of the play, Halie speaks from offstage. She enters for the first time in the middle of this speech, "dressed completely in black, as though in mourning. Black handbag, hat with a veil and pulling on elbow-length black gloves. She is about sixty-five with pure white hair."

HALIE *(From offstage)*: Nobody's going to look after us. Bradley can't look after us. Bradley can hardly look after himself. I was always hoping that Tilden would look out for Bradley when they got older. After Bradley lost his leg. Tilden's the oldest. I always thought he'd be the one to take responsibility. I had no idea in the world that Tilden would be so much trouble. Who would've dreamed. Tilden was an all-American, don't forget. Don't forget that. Fullback. Or quarterback. I forget which. [. . .]

Then when Tilden turned out to be so much trouble, I put all my hopes on Ansel. Of course Ansel wasn't as handsome, but he was smart. He was the smartest probably. I think he probably was. Smarter than Bradley, that's for sure. Didn't go and chop his leg off with a chain saw. Smart enough not to go and do that. I think he was smarter than Tilden too. Especially after Tilden got in all that trouble. Doesn't take brains to go to jail. Anybody knows that. Course then when Ansel passed that left us all alone. Same as being alone. No different. Same as if they'd all died. He was the smartest. He could've earned lots of money. Lots and lots of money. *(Halie enters from the top of the staircase as she continues talking)*

He would've took care of us too. He would've seen to it that we were repaid. He was like that. He was a hero. Don't forget that. A genuine hero. Brave. Strong. And very intelligent. [. . .] Ansel could've been a great man. One of the greatest. I only regret that he didn't die in action. It's not fitting for a man like that to die in a motel room. A soldier. He could've won a medal. He could've been decorated for valor. I've talked to Father Dewis about putting up a plaque for Ansel. He thinks it's a good idea. He agrees. He knew Ansel when he used to play basketball. Went to every game. Ansel was his favorite player. He even recommended to the City Council that they put up a statue of Ansel. A big, tall statue with a basketball in one hand and a rifle in the other. That's how much he thinks of Ansel. [. . .]

Of course, he'd still be alive today if he hadn't married into the Catholics. The Mob. How in the world he never opened his eyes to that is beyond me. Just beyond me. Everyone around him could see the truth. Even Tilden. Tilden told him time and again. Catholic women are the Devil incarnate. He wouldn't listen. [. . .] He was blind with love. Blind. I knew. Everyone knew. The wedding was more like a funeral. You remember? All those Italians. All that horrible black, greasy hair. The rancid smell of cheap cologne. I think even the priest was wearing a pistol. When he gave her the ring I knew he was a dead man. I knew it. As soon as he gave her the ring. But then it was the honeymoon that killed him. The honeymoon. I knew he'd never come back from the honeymoon.

THE COLORED MUSEUM

By George C. Wolfe

The Colored Museum *is set in "a museum where the myths and madness of black/Negro/colored Americans are stored." In this biting and exuberant satire, the characters—who are the "exhibits"—must navigate between recognizing the pain caused by a legacy of oppression without being defined by it in the present. In the "Permutations" exhibit, we meet Normal Jean Reynolds. She is, Wolfe writes, "very southern/country and very young. She wears a simple, faded print dress and her hair, slightly mussed, is in plaits. Between her legs is a very large white egg."*

NORMAL: My mama used to say, God made the exceptional, then God made the special, and when God got bored, he made me. Course she don't say too much of nuthin no more, not since I lay me this egg. Ya see it all got started when I had me sexual relations with the garbage man. Ooowee did he smell. No, not bad. No! He smelled of all the good things folks never shoulda thrown away. His sweat was like cantaloupe juice. His neck was like a ripe-red strawberry. And the water that fell from his eyes was like a deep, dark, juicy-juicy grape. I tell ya, it was like fuckin a fruit salad, only I didn't spit out the seeds. I kept them here, deep inside. And three days later, my belly commence to swell, real big like.

Well my mama locked me off in some dark room, refusin to let me see light of day 'cause "What would the neighbors think." At first I cried a lot, but then I grew used to livin my days in the dark, and my nights in the dark . . . *(She hums)* And then it wasn't but a week or so later, my mama off at church, that I got this hurtin feeling down here. Worse than anything I'd ever known. And then I started bleedin, real bad. I mean there was blood everywhere. And the pain had me howlin like a near-dead dog. I tell ya, I was yellin so loud,

I couldn't even hear myself. Noooooooo! Noooooo! Carrying on something like that. And I guess it was just too much for the body to take, 'cause the next think I remember . . . is me coming to and there's this big white egg layin 'tween my legs. First I thought somebody musta put it there as some kind of joke. But then I noticed that all round this egg were thin lines of blood that I could trace to back between my legs.

(Laughing) Well, when my mama come home from church she just about died. "Normal Jean, what's that thing 'tween your legs? Normal Jean you answer me girl!" It's not a thing Mama. It's an egg. And I laid it. She tried separatin me from it, but I wasn't havin it. I stayed in that dark room, huggin, holdin onto it. *(She hums)* And then I heard it. It wasn't anything that coulda been heard round the world, or even in the next room. It was kinda like layin back in the bathtub, ya know, the water just coverin your ears . . . and if you lay real still and listen real close, you can hear the sound of your heart movin in the water. You ever done that? Well that's what it sounded like. A heart movin water. And it was happenin inside here.

Why I'm the only person I know who ever lay themselves an egg before so that makes me special. You hear that Mama? I'm special and so's my egg! And special things supposed to be treated like they matter. That's why every night I count to it, so it knows nuthin never really ends. And I sing it every song I know so that when it comes out, it's full of all kinds of feelings. And I tell it secrets and laugh with it and . . . *(She suddenly stops, puts her ear to the egg and listens intently)* Oh! I don't believe it! I thought I heard . . . yes! *(Excited)* Can you hear it? Instead of one heart, there's two. Two little hearts just pattering away. Boom-boom-boom. Boom-boom-boom. Talkin to each other like old friends. Racin toward the beginning of their lives. *(Listening)* Oh no now there's three . . . four . . . five, six, more hearts than I can count. And they're all alive, beatin out life inside my egg. *(We begin to hear light drumming, the heartbeats inside Normal's egg)*

Any day now, this egg is gonna crack open and what's gonna come out a be the likes of which nobody has ever seen. My babies! And their skin is gonna turn all kinds of shades in the sun and their hair a be growin every whichaway. And it won't matter and they won't care 'cause they know they are so rare and so special 'cause it's not every day a bunch of babies break outta a white egg and start to live.

And nobody better not try and hurt my babies 'cause if they do, they gonna have to deal with me. Yes any day now, this shell's gonna crack and my babies are gonna fly. Fly! Fly! *(She laughs at the thought, but then stops and says the word as if it's the most natural thing in the world)* Fly.

4

"HAPPIER EVER AFTER . . ."

THE WAITING ROOM

By Lisa Loomer

Lisa Loomer on Wanda: "A modern gal from New Jersey. Forty. Enormous breasts and perfected everything else, too . . . Wanda has watched too much Marilyn Monroe." In this first monologue, Wanda has just been told that she has a tumor in her breast that may be malignant. She heads to a bar across the street from the hospital, and describes a bet she made with her mother five years earlier.

WANDA: I got home last night, I had six calls on my machine. Four of 'em from guys. [. . .] I joined this video-dating thing. One's an extremely handsome, sensitive CEO who makes time for his many friends. One's in construction, but he likes long walks in the rain . . . One's a Christian, and he only dates women between five-eight and six-one, which I don't think is very Christian of him, and they gotta be blond but he'll consider a dyed blond who accepts Jesus . . . *(Thrilled)* And the last guy's a smoker. [. . .] Plus, he doesn't want kids, he lives in Manhattan, he likes to eat in restaurants, which is where I like to eat, and he doesn't jog. So, I figure as long as he doesn't have bad breath, a record, or a fish on his car, this is it. The bet's up in thirty days. This is the guy. [. . .]

Don't you want to know about the bet? [. . .] I'll have another. [. . .] See, I made a bet with my mother five years ago after I read this article she sent me from *Newsweek* while I was waiting to get a Pap smear. [. . .] The article said the odds of my getting married by forty were not quite as good as the odds of my being shot by a terrorist. I wonder how come these articles never mention the possibility of a terrorist falling madly in love and wanting to marry you? [. . .] So anyway, I bet my mother a hundred bucks I'd beat the odds, and I went to work. [. . .] Damn straight. I saw this modeling expert who said to divide my body in parts and go over it with a magnifying glass. Parts I could improve, I'd work on, and the rest I'd just cover up. So I started from the top. Hair, eyebrows— [. . .] Man, you should have seen the Visa bills. Luckily, I had a couple of boyfriends along the way who were very . . . supportive, if not marriage material. [. . .]

So then I went to work on my weight. I did Jenny Craig, Weight Watchers, Nutrisystem, Optifast, Jenny Craig, cocaine and finally lipo. Then I met this writer in a bar who did an article on me and the bet for *Self* magazine, and the most beautiful thing started happening. Women all over the country started sending me donations. I got on *Oprah*, Great Expectations gave me a lifetime membership, I even got a letter from my local councilman—it was like, hey, even the government wants me to win! The Paramus Kiwanis Club wants to give me their hall for my wedding—the Vanity Fair Outlet is gonna give me a trousseau, Video Nuts is giving me and my husband a free membership, and the Taj Mahal in Atlantic City is donating the bridal suite! So now I got thirty days to find the guy, and this morning I went to the doctor . . . and I got a tumor. *(Beat; drinks)* And that's how I'm doing.

THE WAITING ROOM

By Lisa Loomer

From the final scene of the play. Wanda reads a traditional fairy tale to another character until she decides to make up her own bedtime story.

WANDA: . . . But Snow White's wicked old stepmother was also bidden to the wedding feast, and when she went to the mirror and said, "Mirror, mirror on the wall, who is the fairest of us all?" the mirror answered, "O Queen, although you are of beauty rare, the young bride is a thousand times more fair." And when the old Queen saw the bride, she knew her for Snow White, and could not stir from the place for terror. And they had red-hot iron shoes ready for her, in which the old Queen had to dance and dance . . . until she fell down dead. *(Pause)* And Snow White and the Prince lived happily ever after. *(Thinks)* If you're young and beautiful, some old broad's gonna try to knock you off. And if you're ugly or old, you're screwed. These Grimm boys got you coming and going. [. . .]

Okay. Once upon a time there were three sisters. All of them stupid. One thought her feet were too big, one thought her waist was too big, and the really stupid one thought her tits weren't big *enough*. So they went to a Magician and said, "Make us perfect." And he held up a magic mirror which made the sisters look like— [. . .]

Okay. And the Magician said, "You too can look just like this." And the sisters gave him a pile of gold, and the Magician worked his magic . . . and built a new tennis court with their money. But, after a few years, the magic started to . . . go bad. [. . .] And the sisters went back to the Magician and he said, "Hey, I said I'd make you perfect, I didn't say you'd be perfect *forever*. Check out the shingle. It says, 'Magician' not 'God.'" And the sisters were really pissed off.

So what did they do? [. . .] First they took all the mirrors in the kingdom and smashed 'em . . . and recycled the glass. Then they told all their girlfriends and daughters, "Next time you want to look in a mirror, don't go to the Magician, come to us." And when the women came to check out their thighs and their noses and all their other problems, they had to look in the sisters' eyes. And the sisters would say, "Oh, gimme a break, you look fine." At first the women didn't believe them, 'cause who believes you when you tell 'em they look good, right? But the sisters kept saying, "You're beautiful" . . . [. . .]

And eventually the women started to buy it. And the Magicians were doing such a lousy business that they all had to move to . . . Europe. It was like magic. Everybody got kissed, and the women who felt like it got married. And the ones who didn't got good jobs in the kingdom. *(Realizes)* And some got both. And everybody lived a whole lot happier ever after.

IN THE BLOOD

By Suzan-Lori Parks

In this modern-day retelling of The Scarlet Letter, *Hester, La Negrita is a single mother with not one but five illegitimate children, and the society that condemns her is contemporary urban America. Early in the play, Hester tells her children— her "five treasures, five joys"—a bedtime story. This is her answer to every child's question, though it is here unspoken: Where did I come from?*

Note: the "(Rest)," an aspect of what Parks understatedly calls her use of "slightly unconventional theatrical elements," signifies "a little time, a pause, a breather," a transition for the actor and the character.

There were once these five brothers and they were all big and strong and handsome and didnt have a care in the world. One was known for his brains so they called him Smarts and one was known for his muscles, so they called him Toughguy, the third one was a rascal so they called him Wild, the fourth one was as goodlooking as all get out and they called him Looker and the fifth was the youngest and they called him Honeychild cause he was as young as he was sweet. And they was always together these five brothers. Everywhere they went they always went together. No matter what they was always together cause they was best friends and wasnt nothing could divide them. And there was this Princess. And she lived in a castle and she was lonesome. She was lonesome and looking for love but she couldnt leave her castle so she couldnt look very far so every day she would stick her head out her window and sing to the sun and every night she would stick her head out and sing to the moon an the stars: "Where are you?" And one day the five brothers heard her and came calling and she looked upon them and she said: "There are five of you, and each one is wonderful and special in his own way. But the law of my country doesnt allow a princess to have more than one husband." And that was such bad news and they were all so in love that they all cried. Until the Princess had an idea. She was after all the Princess, so she changed the law of the land and married them all.

(Rest)

And with Bro Smarts she had a baby named Jabber. And with Bro Toughguy she had Bully. With Bro Wild came Trouble. With Bro Looker she had Beauty. With Bro Honeychild came Baby. And they was all happy.

RECKLESS

By Craig Lucas

The beginning of the play, Christmas Eve. Rachel, the mother of two boys, is at her bedroom window watching the snow fall. Tom, her husband, is in bed watching the television with the sound turned down. Rachel's naïve, blissful joy—what she describes here as a "euphoria attack"—sets the tone for Craig Lucas's dreamlike comic adventure.

RACHEL: I think I'm more excited than they are. I really do. I think we just have kids so we can tell them all about Santa Claus and have an excuse to believe it all ourselves again. I really do. They are so excited. I remember that feeling so clearly. I didn't think I could ever sleep. And I remember pinching myself and pinching myself to stay awake so I could hear the reindeers' footsteps, you know? I wanted to believe it so badly. I think that was the last year I did . . . Oh God . . . Is it still snowing? Why don't you turn the sound up? Oh, it's coming down like crazy. You can hear it, can't you, when it gets deep like this? It just swallows up all the sound and you feel like you've been wrapped up in the hands of a big, sweet, giant, white . . . monster. Good monster. He's going to carry us away into a dream. My family always had champagne first thing before we opened our presents—I mean, in the morning, you know. I always loved that. I felt like such an adult having champagne and I remember saying to my mother that the bubbles in the champagne looked like snow if you turned your head upside down. I remember thinking I wanted to live in Alaska because it always snowed and Santa was up there, so it must always be Christmas . . . You're my Santa Claus. And our two elves. I'm having one of my euphoria attacks. I think I'm going to be terminally happy, you'd better watch out, it's catching. Highly contagious . . .

RECKLESS

By Craig Lucas

Moments after the first monologue from Reckless *(above),
Tom tells Rachel that he has taken a contract out on her life.
Dressed only in a nightgown and slippers, she flees out the
window and into the night. In this monologue, much later in
the play, Rachel describes what happened to her after she ran
away from home and changed her life.*

RACHEL: Well, last Christmas? Christmas Eve? My husband
Tom is all tucked into bed like a little kid and our two boys
are in their beds, I've just tucked them in, and I tell Tom how
perfect it all seems, I've never been so happy, which is true.
And . . . Well, my father was allergic to dogs, you know, and
Tom didn't like puppies, so I never said anything about wanting a puppy but I was thinking about it. And I was looking out
onto the snow and talking about Alaska or something, but
I was thinking about how people in books and movies are
always getting puppies on Christmas and you never see anybody having to clean up the . . . [. . .] Or get hit by cars. You
always see them with a big red bow and the kids are smiling
and—but I didn't say anything, I was just thinking it, I didn't
want Tom to feel guilty if he hadn't gotten me a puppy which
I knew he hadn't because he hates them, so it was just a pri-
vate little something I was thinking about and that's all I needed
really was to think about it and rub its little imaginary ears. And
we were watching the news, I remember, and suddenly I realize
Tom's upset. So naturally I assume he knows I really want a
puppy, so I go to comfort him, because I don't care about it,
really, if it's going to make him unhappy, I don't even mention
it, I just give him a big hug and tell him it's Christmas and be
happy and he says he's taken a contract out on my life. [. . .]
  Maybe I'm overreacting. Or he's kidding, which I think
he must be. But anyway, I wind up spending Christmas with

this man I meet at the Arco station and his girlfriend who is crippled and deaf, she says, you know, with hand signals until suddenly she just turns to me and starts saying how she had to pretend she was deaf to get the attention of this man we're all living with who's changed his name and run away and she's changed her name and I've changed my name and we're all working in the same place and she's telling me all these secrets and all of a sudden she says, "Why don't you talk to a psychiatrist?"

5

"YOU WILL REMEMBER THIS."

TONGUE OF A BIRD

By Ellen McLaughlin

Maxine is a search-and-rescue pilot. She's vulnerable, but only on the inside; the person she shows the world is tough, flinty and determined to succeed at her job, which is to rescue things—and people—that have been lost. The only thing that Maxine cannot do is come to terms with the loss of her own mother. When she was a very little girl, perhaps six or five or four, her mother killed herself—a memory that Maxine has blocked out, to the point where she remembers nothing at all about or even before her mother's death. This is the first speech of the play, our introduction to Maxine, her grief and her obsession with flight.

MAXINE: There's a girl, this is me, standing at a high window, looking down. She tells herself: you will remember this. And I do. I remember everything. But I don't remember why I remember this.

It is morning and I'm looking down across a vast landscape and I've lost something which I think I will spot from this height. The farther up you are the more you see. This is true, I have learned this since. Because it's what I do for a living. I look, from a great height, for what's been lost. I'm a pilot . . . search and rescue. And it's like a flicker of light sometimes, perhaps the glint of climber's goggles, the quirk, almost indiscernible, of the wrong color, the dropped glove, the upturned shoe. These things, the slight, the rare, I see them as others don't, I am gifted—and here something about this memory comes in . . .

A fly, I know, is buzzing up the window, a trapped fly, going up the air which it finds strangely hard and unyielding, going up when it means to be going out. This is crucial but I don't know why. Perhaps it just tells me the season, which must be late autumn, a time when flies are dying in just this way, going up when they mean to be going out. And it seems to me that all nature is dying on this day. Except me, who stands and watches.

So there's the fly and there's the landscape, dropped like a platter below me. I see it as if I were above it, looking down over the back of my own blond head. I see most of my past this way, remembered with a detachment which looks coolly down on the child I am, experiencing some dreadful thing, which I experienced but didn't, and experience again in recalling it, but don't. There is that girl, who is me, so far below me, who might have lived my life if I hadn't left her there and come up here to watch her. *(Smiles)* I was so terribly good at that. A trick I learned so early.

So I became a flyer. But she asked me to remember this. So I look down with her on the bald hills of some uncertain autumn, and we hear the fly and we wait.

THREE TALL WOMEN

By Edward Albee

In the first act of Edward Albee's Pulitzer Prize–winning play, Three Tall Women, *we meet A, "a very old woman"; B, her paid companion, who "looks rather like A would have at 52"; and C, a lawyer, who "looks rather as B would have at 26." In the second act, the three characters appear as one woman at different stages of her life, creating a fugue-like portrait of*

A's long life. In this speech from the first act, A, now near death, tells the others about a long-ago night with her husband.

A: We had been out—I'll never forget it, I'll never forget this— we'd been to a party, and we'd had champagne, and we were . . . what? Tipsy?, a little I suppose. And we came home and we were on the way to bed. We had our big bedroom, and it had its separate dressing rooms, and—you know—its separate bathrooms—and we were undressing; we were getting ready for bed. I was at my table, and I'd take off my clothes—my shoes, my dress, and my underthings—and I was sitting there at my dressing table *(She really enjoys telling this: laughs, giggles, etc.)* and I was . . . well, I was naked. I didn't have a stitch, except I had on all my jewelry. I hadn't taken off my jewelry.

[B: How wonderful!]

A: Yes!, and there I was, all naked with my pearls—my necklace—and my bracelets, my diamond bracelets . . . two, no; three! Three! And in he walked, naked as a jaybird—he was funny when he wanted to be—we were naked a lot, early on, pretty early on. All that stopped. *(Pause)* Where am I?

[B: In your story?]

A: What?

[B: In your story. Where are you in your story?]

A: Yes; of course.

[C: You're naked at your dressing table, and *he* walks in, and *he's* naked, too.]

A: . . . as a jaybird; yes! Oh, I shouldn't *tell* this!

[B: Yes! Yes, you should!
C: Yes!]

A: Yes? Oh . . . well, there I was, and I had my big powder puff, and I was powdering myself, and I was paying attention to *that*. I knew he was there, but I wasn't paying attention. I *have* something for you, he said, I *have* something for you. And I was sitting there, and I raised my eyes and looked in the mirror and . . . no! I can't tell this!

[B AND C *(Silly schoolgirls; ad-lib)*: Yes, yes; tell, tell. Tell us! Yes! Tell us!]

A: And I looked and there he was, and his . . . his pee-pee was all hard, and . . . and hanging on it was a new bracelet.

[C *(Awe)*: Oh, my God!

(B smiles.)]

A: And it was on his pee-pee, and he came close and it was the most beautiful bracelet I'd ever seen; it was diamonds, and it was wide, so wide and . . . I thought you might like this, he said. Oh, my goodness, it's so beautiful, I said. Do you want it? he said. Yes, yes! I said, Oh, goodness, yes! *(Mood shifts a little toward darkness)* And he came closer, and his pee-pee touched my shoulder—he was short, and I was tall, or something. Do you want it? he said, and he poked me with it, with his pee-pee, and I turned, and he had a little pee-pee. Oh, I shouldn't say that; that's terrible to say, but I *know*. He had a little . . . *you* know . . . and there was the bracelet on it, and he moved closer, to my face, and Do you want it? I thought you might like it. And I said, No! I can't *do* that! You *know* I can't *do* that! And I couldn't; I could *never* do that, and I said, No! I can't *do* that! And he stood there for . . . well, I don't know . . . and his pee-pee got . . . well, it started to go soft, and the bracelet slid off, and it fell into my lap. I was naked; deep into my lap. Keep it, he said, and he turned and walked out of my dressing room. *(Long silence; finally she weeps, slowly, conclusively)*

FUDDY MEERS

By David Lindsay-Abaire

Playwright David Lindsay-Abaire describes the central character of his dark comedy as "a generally sunny woman with amnesia." Claire, in her early forties, wakes up every morning without any knowledge of who she is—a protective response to the unsettling, funhouse-like and possibly dangerous world in which she lives. A dog's bark suddenly triggers memories of Nancy, a retriever who used to belong to her neighbor. She tells her mother what she remembers of the day the dog died, when Claire was a child.

CLAIRE: You remember that dog? Skinny old thing Mr. Cuthart kept tied up in the front lawn all day? Daddy always said he was gonna report him. Remember she just sat in the sun, biting at her scabs? Cuthart didn't even give her any water. [. . .] Nancy. So I'd sneak down the road with my squirt gun, and spritz water into her mouth and she'd bark. [. . .] And one day, when Cuthart was downtown, I untied her to let her run around a little. But she darted straight into the road, just as Daddy's pick-up was coming around the curve, and he didn't see her, so he plowed into her. Do you remember Daddy and I came through the back door, Mama? And Nancy was hanging out of his arms like a set of broken-up bagpipes. And he spread her out on the kitchen floor and she was breathing real hard. And the pain was humming off of her like I could hear it. And she just let the pain take her over. And that's all she was. This *pained* thing. And Daddy was bent over her, talking to her real quiet. And all of a sudden Nancy stood up, like it was a new day, and she started running around the kitchen like she wasn't half dead, barking and clicking her nails against the floor tiles. And we were all shocked because Nancy was like a puppy all of a sudden, not that bony heap on the floor. She was this fire ball for about three minutes, until she got tired again, and curled up beside the sink and went to sleep and died like it meant nothing. You remember how all that happened in here? It's funny how almost everything else is gone to me, and that sad old dog just came into my head.

AUGUST SNOW

By Reynolds Price

August Snow *is the first play of Reynolds Price's* New Music *trilogy, which follows the relationship between Neal Avery and his wife Taw from their courtship in Depression-era North Carolina through their maturity, in a generational cycle that spans two generations and forty years. Here, Neal's mother Roma, age forty-three and a widowed housewife, tells the audience about her father.*

ROMA: Till the day he died, my father was the thing I thought loved me. He was young—nineteen the year I was born—and he seldom spoke ten words a day; so he never *told* me, never spoke the word: not *love*, not in my hearing at least. That was fine by me. All this talk of mine—my Famous Fountain of Truth—came after he died.

   Till I was four I spoke not a word and almost never cried, and by then Mother'd told the world I was mute. Father didn't seem to worry a bit but rode me everywhere he went, on his broad English saddle, far out in the country—he managed timber for his great-grandfather, who'd known James Madison when he was a boy.

The winter I was four, we were out near the river, in a noon so bright my eyes stayed shut; and Father spoke for the first time in hours. He said, "Rome, speak now—this precious instant—or nevermore." So my eyes clicked open, and I said plainly, "Let's just keep going on from here." I meant *Not home. Anywhere else but home*, though Mother was a saint almost beyond doubt. Father said not a word but spurred us on. I think he obeyed me, I honestly do, till midafternoon. At least we saw trees we'd never passed before, both of us silent as stones, each step.

Then a moment came when I felt him turn back. I knew because I was happy till then; but once that horse turned home at a jog, I broke like a stick—for good, for life. Just two nights later Father died across town at a girl's back door, shot once by her brother in the midst of his heart in dark thick as fur.

Next morning I commenced normal speech, no tears, with nobody I much cared to address—not then or since. In the last twenty years, I've enjoyed Neal of course. Father shows in his eyes sometimes, in the dusk.

AUGUST SNOW

By Reynolds Price

Twenty-one-year-old Taw Avery was raised in an orphanage and grew up to become a schoolteacher. Married to Neal Avery for just one year, she can already sense him drifting away from her. She describes a dream in what Price calls "an unashamed soliloquy" addressed to the audience.

TAW: Since I was an orphan so early in life, I taught myself to avoid most dreams—dreams at night, good or bad. They seemed one strain I could spare myself; and I honestly think, in all these years, I've never had two dozen dreams—not to speak of. Neal dreams like a dog by the stove when he's here, the rare nights I get to guard his sleep. Last night though when I finally dozed, sad as I was, I lived through a dream as real as day. I'd finished my teacher's diploma and was ready to save the world around me, all children. What thrilled me was *that*—they were all young and not too hard yet to help. I'd show them the main thing an orphan knows—how to tuck your jaw and brave hails of pain and come out strong as a good drayhorse or a rock-ribbed house on a cliff by water. But once I entered my class the first day and trimmed my pencil and faced the desks, I saw they'd given me twenty grown men—all with straight sets of teeth. I prayed I was wrong, that I'd got the wrong room. Still I said my name, and the oldest man at the back of the room stood tall at last in a black serge suit and said, "Don't wait another minute to start. We've paid our way." I had a quick chill of fright that I'd fail; but then I thought of the week they died—my mother and father, of Spanish flu—and I knew I did have a big truth to tell, the main one to know. I opened my mouth and taught those grown men every last fact an orphan needs and learns from the day she's left—courage and trust and a craving for time. They listened too but hard as I looked in all the rows, I never saw Neal.

THE MONOGAMIST

By Christopher Kyle

Sky Hickock is a young college student in 1991. She grew up during twelve years of Republican political dominance and is, as the playwright notes, "politically not-too-into-it." She tries to explain why she voted for George Bush.

SKY: So what I'm saying is . . . What was I saying? Oh, yeah. About the '60s. The '60s were obviously this totally cool decade, you know, where everybody was whacked on some major drugs. And you had Morrison, Hendrix, Janis Joplin—all these fucking heroes—Mick Jagger. Okay? And Vietnam, which wasn't cool really, I guess, but it was definitely something to *care* about, and that's something about which I don't know *shit*. Caring, I mean. I want to get whacked, sure, but there's no . . . political content to it, okay? It's just people getting, you know, totally fucked up and wearing tie-dye shirts. It's a total rip-off of your whole culture and everybody knows it. Okay? Everybody knows it, which is, I guess, why it's cool. It's like totally fake and that's what's . . . *right* about it. It's like, hey—we don't give a shit about anything, but we're hip to it. Nobody's gonna blow us any shit. Nobody's gonna pull anything on us . . . like that Watergate, am I right? I bet that caught you by surprise. Not me. I knew what was going down and I was only *four years old*. It's like politics, you know? It's bogus. This whole country's all just . . . bogus. And that's why I voted for George Bush. [. . .] I mean, the only thing that really *matters*, the only *issue*, is abortion. Okay? I mean, I could march on Washington or some bullshit for that. A woman should be able to choose. Choices—okay?—that's what it's all about. Options. Think about how few choices there used to be at McDonald's. When I was a kid there was, like, hamburger, cheeseburger, fries, shake. That's it. Now it takes half an hour to read the fucking menu. That's options. That's progress.

6

"I CROSSED THE LINE."

IN THE BLOOD

By Suzan-Lori Parks

Suzan-Lori Parks gives each of the adult characters in her modern-day riff on The Scarlet Letter *"confessions," interior monologues that are shared with the audience. A dramatic device for the characters to reveal events that happened off-stage, or in the past, the confessions give a dramatic context to the seemingly good and upright citizens who exploit Hester, La Negrita, and her five illegitimate children. While the word "confessions" implies an unburdening, a revelation of some wrongdoing, these monologues are delivered without apology or shame.*

Note: the "(Rest)," an aspect of what Parks understatedly calls her use of "slightly unconventional theatrical elements," signifies a little time, a pause, a breather, a transition for the actor and the character.

THE WELFARE:
  I walk the line
  between us and them
  between our kind and their kind.
  The balance of the system depends on a well-drawn
      boundary line
  And all parties respecting that boundary
  I am
  I am a married woman
  I dont—that is have never

never in the past or even in the recent present or even
    when I look
look out into the future of my life I do not see any
    interest
any *sexual* interest
in anyone
other than my husband.
(Rest)
My dear husband.
The hours he keeps.
The money he brings home.
Our wonderful children.
The vacations we go on.
My dear husband he needed
a little spice.
And I agreed. We both needed spice.
We both hold very demanding jobs.
We put an ad in the paper: "Husband and Bi-Curious
    Wife, seeking—"
But the women we got:
Hookers. Neurotics. Gold diggers!
"Bring one of those gals home from work," Hubby said.
    And
Hester,
she came to tea.
(Rest)
She came over and we had tea.
From my mothers china.
And marzipan on matching china plates.
Hubby sat opposite in the recliner
hard as Gibraltar. He told us what he wanted and we
    did it.
We were his little puppets.
She was surprised, but consented.
Her body is better than mine.
Not a single stretchmark on her

Im a looker too don't get me wrong just in a different
    way and
Hubby liked the contrast.
Just light petting at first.
Running our hands on each other
then Hubby joined in
and while she and I kissed
Hubby did her and me alternately.
The thrill of it—.
(Rest)
I was so afraid Id catch something
but I was swept away and couldnt stop
She stuck her tongue down my throat
and Hubby doing his thing on top
my skin shivered
She let me slap her across the face
and I crossed the line.
(Rest)
It was my first threesome
and it wont happen again.
And I should emphasize that
she is a low-class person.
What I mean by that is that we have absolutely nothing
    in common.
As her caseworker I realize that maintenance of the sys-
    tem depends on a well-drawn boundary line
and all parties respecting that boundary.
And I am, after all,
I am a married woman.

SILENCE, CUNNING, EXILE

By Stuart Greenman

Inspired by events in the life of photographer Diane Arbus,
Silence, Cunning, Exile *takes place over the course of twenty-one years, from 1950 to 1971, tracing both the evolution and downfall of a photographer named Suzie. We first meet Suzie when she is young, in her early twenties, and working as a fashion photographer in collaboration with her husband, Donald. Like Arbus, Suzie finds her own artistic vision only when she begins to photograph the people on the fringes of society, the underworld of New York City. In this scene, she has shocked her old friend Frank (who was in love with her) by showing him her "new" portfolio for the first time.*

SUZIE: I work a lot, now. I've been working. Ten whole bloody years. There's going to be another show. Isaac's been— [. . .] If I want. In October. [. . .] If I want. And I teach some. [. . .] For the money. [. . .] But I've been working. There are a lot of places to go. That I—I have to go to them. Sometimes it's like an appointment book, and it's so full. I didn't make the appointments, but I have them, I have to keep them.

I met a woman on the bus, Betty, she was fifty-five. "My," she said, "what a lot of equipment for such a little girl." [. . .] She looked like my best friend Sarah's mother when I was eight, except this woman had white hair. She worked as a foundation-garments saleswoman. She showed me pictures of her sons, Mark and Joey. Joey had freckles, a real redhead but such a sunny disposition, whereas Mark . . . And we got to her place, a little yellow bungalow in Rockaway, and down in the basement, well, it's all finished like a rec room, with walnut paneling that her husband, Jimmy, had put up before he passed away, and Betty had this glass breakfront down there. She opens it up and shows me her knickknacks, which happen to be these incredible nipple clips with rhinestones, and this penis ring, and this enormous black dildo, and I say ooh, and oh, and that's nice, and she smiles and puts them all away again. Then we go upstairs for tea. And she says Mr. Lucas is coming over later, she usually just calls him Karl, but he's very nice, would I care to meet him? And I say . . . [. . .] Oh! I forgot! On the middle shelf of the breakfront is a collection of porcelain bathtubs, you know, from different vacation spots: "We had a tub of fun in Miami."

I made love to Karl, and Betty took our picture. I've made love to a hunchback. I've made—. On a Greyhound bus, if you're available, you sit on the inside back seat.

THREE HOTELS

By Jon Robin Baitz

Barbara Hoyle's husband, Kenneth, designed a baby-formula marketing policy in the Third World for an international conglomerate—a company that is, in Barbara's words, "a perpetrator of an evil." After their sixteen-year-old son Brandon was stabbed to death, Kenneth R. Hoyle was given this job because, Barbara says, "he had, after Brandon died in Rio, turned to stone and could do anything" without caring about the moral implications or consequences. In this excerpt, part of a long monologue addressed to the audience, Barbara describes a speech she delivered at a company conference—a talk that would, as a result, "deep-six" Kenneth's career "in one magnificent end run."

BARBARA: This morning I gave a speech to a group of wives. "Wives of Executives Stationed in the Third World. Barbara Hoyle, wife of Kenneth R. Hoyle (formerly of the Peace Corps)." Every two years my husband's company has this conference— a sort of baby formula summit. I couldn't go to the last two.

Which, Ken let it be known, was a hardship on him. [. . .] Ken told me there were some grumblings, so I knew I'd have to go this year and so I really did my homework and prepared and it's not so bad.

(Beat.)

But to tell you the truth, I was very shaky, I was really in trouble. My speech to the young wives assigned to the Third World—the 3-W club, they call it—they have a little newsletter. I used to even write for it now and then when we were in Brazil. Mostly recipes—that's all they wanted really was mostly recipes and shopping hints.

(Beat.)

My speech was entitled BE CAREFUL. Simply BE CAREFUL. [. . .] I say this to them and I mean it, I want to help. "Be careful of spending too much time alone. Learn the language— whatever you do—learn the language fast. The silence in those houses they find for you with the servants—it can overwhelm you." I smile. A sister. "Look, I'm gonna level with you,"— now I know I'm really hitting my stride, doing a sort of a midwife routine—"they say it's an adventure and it is. But it's also a sacrifice. You're giving up things here and when you come back, it'll never be the same—make sure your husband understands this. Make sure he knows that what you're coming back to is not the . . ."

(Pause.)

"Of course, not all of you will come back with a dead son."

(Beat. She smiles sadly.)

Have I crossed a line? I never talk about this. But it seems false—mealy-mouthed not to make mention of it—and I—to tell you the truth—I am beginning to realize it is expected of me. I go on. "Most likely, percentage-wise very few of you will come back without a child—but if you . . . come back . . . with a coffin . . .

(Beat.)

"Talk about it." They nod. They *know.* They're women for God's sake, not just DARs. I shake my head. "You know—we hear the news. 'We're moving overseas.' Maybe we're sitting in the kitchen alone after they've gone to the office, having that quiet cup of afternoon coffee and the phone rings and it's your husband and he says, 'I was right. We're going to . . . Surinam or Sri Lanka or *Rio.*' And there is this sense of . . . 'oh, it's a mission . . .' that sort of overtakes you. A dream.

"Remember, it is not . . . your mission. Your husband's mission is not—your mission. Be careful . . . that you keep the clarity of your own life." I pause. They are nodding. "Or you will come back and you will have . . . dust. You will have nothing." Silence.

7

"DO YOU KNOW WHO I AM?"

STOP KISS

By Diana Son

Callie, in her late twenties to early thirties, is someone who "swerves" through life—she panics when it comes to making a decision, let alone a commitment. Then she meets Sara, a recent arrival to New York and, tentatively, their friendship blossoms into romance. When Sara is severely beaten in a gay-bashing incident and Callie is labeled as a lesbian—a label she herself is not ready to accept—she is forced to examine, perhaps for the first time, who she is and what she wants. She delivers this speech to Sara, who is still in a coma, in the hospital.

CALLIE: They're finished building that building across from your apartment.

(Sara doesn't respond.)

(Conversational volume) Wake up now.

(No response.)

(A little stronger) Sara.

(No response.)

Can you hear me? *(Nothing)* Open your eyes.

(No response.)

Open your eyes.

(No response.)

They're gonna start you on physical therapy tomorrow. Just little stuff, range of motion, something to get your blood moving. *(Pause)* You've gotten all these cards and letters, I'll read some to you later. *(Pause)* You know your parents are here. They're doing their best—I think they're doing OK, considering. You getting better makes them feel better—yeah. *(Pause)* They look at me . . . your parents look at me . . . like I'm some dirty old man. *(She waits for a response)* And the newspapers, the TV, the radio—my station, my own station, when they ran the news about the attack, they identified me—"Traffic reporter for this station." Now everybody—the guy at the deli—I used to be the blueberry-muffin lady, now I'm the lesbian traffic reporter whose lover got beat up. And I've gotten letters—from two women, their girlfriends were *killed* during attacks—and they wrote me these heartbreaking letters telling me what they've been through . . . and they tell me to speak truth to power and I don't know what that *means*, Sara. Do you? Do you know me? Do you know who I am?

(Sara opens her eyes.)

THE COLORED MUSEUM

By George C. Wolfe

The Colored Museum *is set in "a museum where the myths and madness of black/Negro/colored Americans are stored." At the start of the play, in the "Git on Board" "exhibit," a perky stewardess named Miss Pat welcomes the audience aboard the "Celebrity Slaveship" —and introduces us, unequivocally, to George C. Wolfe's sharp, satirical look at black culture and history.*

MISS PAT: Welcome aboard Celebrity Slaveship, departing the Gold Coast and making short stops at Bahia, Port-au-Prince and Havana, before our final destination of Savannah.

Hi, I'm Miss Pat and I'll be serving you here in Cabin A. We will be crossing the Atlantic at an altitude that's pretty high, so you must wear your shackles at all times.

(Removes a shackle from the overhead compartment and demonstrates) To put on your shackle, take the right hand and close the metal ring around your left hand like so. Repeat the action using your left hand to secure the right. If you have any trouble bonding yourself, I'd be more than glad to assist.

Once we reach the desired altitude, the captain will turn off the "Fasten Your Shackle" sign . . . allowing you a chance to stretch and dance in the aisles a bit. But otherwise, shackles must be worn at all times.

Also, we ask that you please refrain from call-and-response singing between cabins as that sort of thing can lead to rebellion. And of course, no drums are allowed on board. Can you repeat after me, "No drums." With a little more enthusiasm, please. "No drums." That was great.

Once we're airborne, I'll be by with magazines, and earphones can be purchased for the price of your first-born male.

If there's anything I can do to make this middle passage more pleasant, press the little button overhead and I'll be with you faster than you can say, "Go down Moses." *(She laughs at her "little joke")* Thanks for flying Celebrity and here's hoping you have a pleasant takeoff.

THE COLORED MUSEUM

By George C. Wolfe

In the opening monologue from The Colored Museum *(above), George C. Wolfe invites the audience to wear their "shackles" at all times. In this, the final speech of the play, he throws them off through the character of Topsy Washington, a "hurricane of energy" who reclaims both the joy and pain of African-American history—the power of her "colored contradictions." Near the end of the speech, the other characters, the "exhibits," come to life and join Topsy onstage in "The Party," creating a cacophony through which Topsy sings.*

TOPSY *(Dancing about)*: Yo-ho! Party! Party! Turn up the music! Turn up the music!

Have yaw ever been to a party where there was one fool in the middle of the room, dancing harder and yelling louder than everybody in the entire place. Well hunny that fool was me!

Yes child! My name is Topsy Washington and I love to party. As a matter of fact, when God created the world, on the seventh day, he didn't rest. No child, he partied! Yo-ho! Party! Yeah! Yeah!

But now let me tell you 'bout this function I went to the other night, way uptown. And baby when I say uptown, I mean way-way-way-way-way-way-way-way uptown. Somewhere between 125th Street and infinity.

Inside was the largest gathering of black/Negro/colored Americans you'd ever want to see. Over in one corner you got Nat Turner sippin champagne out of Eartha Kitt's slipper. And over in another corner, Bert Williams and Malcolm X was discussing existentialism as it related to the shuffle-ball-change. Girl, Aunt Jemima and Angela Davis was in the kitchen sharing a plate of greens and just goin off about South Africa.

And then Fats sat down and started to work them eighty-eights. And then Stevie joined in. And then Miles and

Duke and Ella and Jimi and Charlie and Sly and Lightnin' and Count and Louie!

And then everybody joined in. I tell you all the children was just all up in there, dancing to the rhythm of one beat. Dancing to the rhythm of their own definition. Celebrating in their cultural madness.

And then the floor started to shake. And the walls started to move. And before anybody knew what was happening, the entire room lifted up off the ground. The whole place just took off and went flying through space—defying logic and limitations. Just a spinning and a spinning and a spinning until it disappeared inside of my head.

(Topsy stops dancing and regains her balance and begins to listen to the music in her head. Slowly we begin to hear it, too.)

That's right girl, there's a party going on inside of here. That's why when I walk down the street my hips sashay all over the place. 'Cause I'm dancing to the music of the madness in me.

And whereas I used to jump into a rage anytime anybody tried to deny who I was, now all I got to do is give attitude, quicker than light, and then go on about the business of being me. 'Cause I'm dancing to the music of the madness in me.

And here all the time I been thinking we gave up our drums. But naw', we still got 'em. I know I got mine. They're here, in my speech, my walk, my hair, my God, my style, my smile and my eyes. And everything I need to get over in this world, is inside here, connecting me to everybody and everything that's ever been.

So hunny don't waste your time trying to label or define me.

. . . 'cause I'm not what I was ten years ago
or ten minutes ago.
I'm all of that and then some.
And whereas I can't live inside yesterday's pain,
I can't live without it.

BURIED CHILD

By Sam Shepard

Shelly, nineteen and very beautiful, has gone with her boyfriend, Vince, to see his family after many years of separation. She doesn't hold much faith in reunions herself, she says, but it's something Vince wanted to do. Trouble is no one recognizes Vince when they get there, and his family begins to seem increasingly unstable. Shelly's response is to fight back; she takes the wooden leg that belongs to Vince's uncle, an amputee, and holds it "as though she's kidnapped it" during this speech.

SHELLY: Don't come near me! Don't anyone come near me. I don't need any words from you. I'm not threatening anybody. I don't even know what I'm doing here. You all say you don't remember Vince, okay, maybe you don't. Maybe it's Vince that's crazy. Maybe he's made this whole family thing up. I don't even care anymore. I was just coming along for the ride. I thought it'd be a nice gesture. Besides, I was curious. He made all of you sound familiar to me. Every one of you. For every name, I had an image. Every time he'd tell me a name, I'd see the person. In fact, each of you was so clear in my mind that I actually believed it was you. I really believed that when I walked through that door that the people who lived here would turn out to be the same people in my imagination. Real people. People with faces. But I don't recognize any of you. Not one. Not even the slightest resemblance.

RECKLESS

By Craig Lucas

In this emotionally resonant dark comedy, Pooty, Lloyd and Rachel have all left their homes, assumed new identities and begun new lives. The audience meets Pooty ("the one and only Pooty-Poot-Pooter") when her boyfriend, Lloyd, introduces her to Rachel, the play's heroine. The audience believes (as does Lloyd) that Pooty, a paraplegic, is deaf and dumb. Here, the first time she speaks in the play, Pooty reveals to Rachel something else entirely.

POOTY: When I lost the use of my legs a friend drove me up here to Springfield to take a look at this place where they worked with the handicapped. I watched the physical therapists working with the patients and there was one; I remember he was working with a quadriplegic. I thought he was the most beautiful man I'd ever seen. A light shining out through his skin. And I thought if I couldn't be with him I'd die. But I knew I would just be one more crippled dame as far as he was concerned, so my friend helped to get me registered as deaf and disabled. I used to teach sign language to the hearing impaired. I thought if I were somehow needier than the rest I would get special attention. I realized soon enough: everyone gets special attention where Lloyd is concerned. But by then it was too late. He was in love with me, with my honesty. He learned to sign; he told me how he'd run away from a bad marriage and changed his name so he wouldn't have to pay child support. He got me a job at Hands Across the Sea and I couldn't bring myself to tell him that I had another name and another life, that I'd run away too, because I owed the government so much money and wasn't able to pay after the accident. I believe in honesty. I believe in total honesty. And I need him and he needs me to be the person he thinks I am and I am that person, I really am that person. I'm a crippled deaf girl, short and stout. Here is my wheelchair, here is my mouth. [. . .]

When he goes out I babble. I recite poetry I remember from grade school. I talk back to the television. I even call people on the phone and say it's a wrong number just to have a conversation. I'm afraid I'm going to open my mouth to scream one day and . . . *(She does; no sound)*

THE DAY ROOM

By Don DeLillo

Nothing is what it seems in novelist Don DeLillo's first play. The first act is set in a hospital, where doctors and nurses tend to patients—until it begins to appear that the doctors and nurses are patients themselves, on the loose from the hospital's Arno Klein Psychiatric Wing. The second act is set in the Klein Wing's day room, a large white space flooded in harsh fluorescent light where "everything's dangerous . . . people say things out of nowhere." Within moments, however, the day room is transformed into a smallish motel room, and we meet a new group of characters that are seeking the elusive Arno Klein theatre—a company that is reputed to perform brilliantly, travels internationally, but just might be a "never-ending rumor." Jolene, a member of the Arno Klein troupe, appears late in DeLillo's play and disappears just as quickly.

She delivers the following monologue in response to another character who has glorified the actor's life, "the words alone . . . the speeches . . ."

JOLENE: I hate speeches. Look. Let me put it this way. When an athlete dies young, it's a terrible twist of nature. Something incoherent trails the event. We're left a little stunned. This boy or girl is a demon runner. Let her run. Let him jump his hurdles. It's all so innocent and bright. How different for an actor, young, old, ancient, budding, decrepit. Dying is what he's all about. We can't be surprised. We know he's been clinging all along. Testing the levels. How far down can he go? How many people can he be? How well can he hide? He develops techniques to shield him from the facts. But they become the facts. He works through his own shallow panic and comes up against deep panic. The basic state. There's no innocence here. Just secrets, terrors, compulsions, deceptions. That's all I have to say. I've said too much. It's too damn grim.

The actor is horribly open to the true state of things. We're forever taking on and shedding protection. We cling, we give in, we hang on, we submit. We can't meet death on our own terms. We have no terms. Our speeches rattle in our throats. We're robbed of all consolations. We're fully aware and completely helpless. We're borderline from the day we're born. Our only hope is other people. A trickle, a sprinkling, sitting here and there, day or night, pale, still, plainfaced, waiting. But the parts we play in order to live make us tremble in our own skin. We're transparent. This is our mystery, our beauty, our genius, our sickness. A play is a secret we all share. According to Klein.

We go on tonight, an hour from now, in a hospital right here in town. The psychiatric wing. There's a room called the day room. They don't use it at night. We've arranged to borrow it, transform it, do our play, disappear. Now you know.

8

"IT'S MY FATE, DO YOU SEE? THIS LOVE."

THE THREE SISTERS

By Anton Chekhov
Adapted by David Mamet

The event of this monologue—Masha's confession of love for Vershinin, the married solider who has been conscripted in her provincial town, so far from Moscow—is pure Chekhov. The style—the pauses, the emphasis, the declarative language—is pure David Mamet.

MASHA: My Sisters? My Clown Soul. My Jolly Soul is heavy, do you want to know? It is. Hear my confession. For I am in torment and my Guilty Knowledge sears my Heart. My sinful Mystery. My secret which screams to be told. I am in love and I love someone. I love a man. You have just seen him. The man that I love. Vershinin. [. . .] What am I to do? You tell me. He was *strange* to me. At first. I *thought* about him. Often. I felt sorry for him. I . . . I "grew to love him." I did. I grew to love him. His *voice* . . . his *ways* . . . his *misfortunes* . . . his two little *girls* . . . [. . .]

You won't hear it? Olga? You won't hear it? Why? I love him. He loves me. It's my Fate, do you see? This love. It's as simple as that. Yes. Yes, it's frightening. Yes. But it's *mine*. It's what I *am*. Yes. My darling. Yes. It's *life* s'what it is. We *live* it, and look what it does to us. We read a novel, and it's clear. It's so *spelled* out. This *isn't* clear. *Nothing* is clear. And *no* one has a final *true* idea of anything. It's "life." We have to *decide*. Each of us. We. Have. To *DECIDE*: what *is*, what it *means*, what we *want*. My darling sisters. *(Pause)* That's what the thing is. And now I've confessed. And I'll be silent. *(Pause)* As the grave. *(Pause)* Silence.

BALLAD OF YACHIYO

By Philip Kan Gotanda

At age sixteen, Yachiyo has been sent away from the place she grew up, a Japanese plantation on the island of Kauai, Hawaii, to learn traditional Japanese arts. Her parents want her to have a better life, meet a man with better prospects than her boyfriend, Willie, a young worker. Instead, Yachiyo begins an affair, which she describes here, with Takamura, the older married man in whose home she is living and being educated.

Philip Kan Gotanda's play, set in 1919, is based on the life of his own aunt, who killed herself after becoming pregnant by her lover.

YACHIYO: His skin was not smooth like Willie's. It was both coarse and smooth. His face, his hands were rough. But under his arm, the back side of his thigh, his skin was like a little boy's. I would run my fingers over those places and he would laugh because it tickled him and his joy would fill me with childish pleasure and I would feel like a little girl gorging on overripe mango. But when I touched his stomach he would grow quiet and the laughter would become thick with musty, sweet odors. And I could feel my own breath growing heavy, the air inside me a prickly heat and I would want his sex, now hard in my hand, to carry me on its swollen current, drowning beneath dark wet fingers.

When I look in the mirror, I cannot see myself the way I used to. Just me, my face looking back at me. My own thoughts, my own feelings. I can only see myself through his eyes now.

How does he see this face? How do I look to him? Am I pretty enough? I cannot tell where my face ends and his eyes begin. And when he touches me, I want his hands to grow into my body, sending roots deep into my flesh. Each touch a new root pushing into the deepest part of me, taking hold, growing into a tangle around the wound that is my heart so we would always be together, nothing could ever separate us.

I am in pain and yet it is so pleasurable. At times I cannot think, I cannot breathe. And to be apart from him for even an instant feels as if time has stopped and I am only waiting, waiting. Until he is there again and I can breathe. I wish it would stop, this feeling. I wish it would never end.

THE CHEMISTRY OF CHANGE

By Marlane Meyer

Lee, the matriarch of a large family, is in her fifties; she's "vain and self-possessed, glamorous." She might have been Miss Salt Lake City when she was younger, but instead of realizing her dream of going to Hollywood, she went into the "marriage business," bringing home a succession of husbands. This speech is in response to her daughter Corlis's statement that Lee hates men: "That's what we all have in common, our common hatred of men," after Lee brings home yet another new partner, Smokey.

    Note: Dixon is Lee's sister; Farley is one of her sons.

LEE: No. I've been thinking about this. See, I got into the habit of saying I hated men because it relieved the tension I'd feel when I was young and I would be dependent on them and they would disappoint me. Hating them was much easier than confronting them and fighting it. Talking to them was nearly impossible so I made them the enemy. And well, frankly, they can be so dense, some of them. And I had you and Dixon to talk to about how men were so awful. And it was so much fun, remember? But then Mr. Farley, you remember Farley's father Mr. Farley . . . ? *(Confessing)* I really liked him. [. . .] After that I swore next time would be different and it was. I steeled myself against my emotions. But then I found myself lying in bed at night wishing these poor jerks, my husbands, would die. Not just leave, but die. Fortunately, they never did, I would have felt awful. No, they'd leave, sometimes with a speech, sometimes with a note in the middle of the night . . . but what a relief, remember the parties we used to have? How drunk we'd all get. But now all that's changed. I think about this Smokey all the time. I look forward to the end of the day when we can be alone, when everyone goes to sleep and it's our time to be with each other . . . Smokey says that night is the oyster and sex is the pearl and this is the treasure of love. If any other man would have said this to me I'd have puked on their shoes. But now I get this queer feeling like I'm growing a flower from the center of my heart.

LLOYD'S PRAYER

By Kevin Kling

Mom and Dad (Hank) are the adoptive parents of Bob, a boy who was raised by raccoons. Encouraging Bob to seek the love of a sweetheart, Mom reveals something of her own unhappiness.

MOM: Bob? What's the matter, honey. Why so down, sweetheart? I know. You're lonely. Don't try and tell me different because I've seen the look before. You bet I have. You think no one loves you because you're different. Right? Am I right? Of course I am. I am right. Well you're wrong. I love you. But that's not what you mean, is it. You need the love of someone your own age. A sweetheart. A mate. Someone who will see you for what you are, a real man, a sex machine, a throbbing magnet of manhood, right? Am I right? Of course I am. But Mom, who could fall for a man with hair all over his back. Believe me Bob they're out there. I'll tell you a little secret. Your father has hair all over his back and I fell for him. That's right. One day, Bob, when you're older, and we let you out of your cage, you'll go to a dance. A veritable symphony of crepe paper and helium. The girls in their taffeta dresses they'll keep forever and never wear again. The boys in airtight outfits counting the holes in the tops of the wingtips. One hole for every place they'd rather be. This is your season of rapture, Bob, your time to dance the wild draining dance of youth. You scan the room and suddenly you're transfixed by a pair of luminous green eyes and . . . Several seconds pass, a glorious eternity. You ask her to dance and soon your face is buried in the scented thickness of her hair. You whisper her name softly and she quivers as your arms of steel wrap around her yielding flesh. As the dance ends you kiss her at first unhurried and then hard and full on the lips sending wave after wave of pulsating pleasures releasing fires she never knew she had. You her strength, her desire. You her hairy-backed Adonis. And she'll follow you anywhere, Bob. Even to a ranch-style home where she'll live entirely without want for fifteen years. Until one day she is put into treatment for God knows why and rises up from the ashes and dumps you for her therapist, Lois, and goes back to school and writes a best-seller and goes on TV and joins with her sisters and sometimes even misses your stupid hairy back. Hank . . . oh Hank.

AUGUST SNOW

By Reynolds Price

Genevieve Slappy, twenty-two, loves Wayne Watkins, who loves her right back but shows no signs of proposing. In 1937 North Carolina, she's at age to marry, but despite Wayne's slowness to propose, she defies unhappiness with patience rather than anger. This speech, addressed to the audience, describes how she came to own her own home, in which she lives as resident landlady.

GENEVIEVE: I'm the youngest property-owner I know—this whole house is mine. Mother left it to me, when my brother Dillard and his big family were jammed in a one-story match-box on the hot side of town. She hoped I would sit here, quiet—renting rooms for the rest of my life—and forget Wayne Watkins and the dream of marriage. I don't under-stand. She and my father were happy together as any two ducks on a deep warm pond. Many times as a child I woke in the night and heard them laughing in the dark down the hall. But when my father died, Mother—young as she was—just started shrinking day by day till the night she vanished. Or so I recall it. She never warned me off men or low-rated love till the evening she left us. Then that night, in the back bedroom, I took in her supper; and she said, "Sit still while I tell you what's true." I sat by her knees, and she said, "Stop waiting by the door like a dog." I said, "Beg your pardon?" She shut her eyes and waited and then said, "I'll pardon you when you can stand alone." I'd been walking unaided from the age of ten months—it bowed my knees slightly—and I reminded her of that. I also mentioned how she'd leaned on Papa those twenty-eight good years. She didn't give an inch but turned her face to the wall, the picture she'd painted as a girl—of buffalo—and she said, "Then I can't pardon you tonight, can I?" I laughed,

"No ma'am. Wait till breakfast tomorrow." And she died before day—leaving me all this, as I said: *(Gestures around)* my life. So she hoped anyhow. She may yet prevail. It is a strong house—heartwood beams and floors.

9

"ART WAS NOT A PART OF OUR LIVES."

BOBRAUSCHENBERGAMERICA

By Charles L. Mee

Bob's Mom is one of many disparate, seemingly unconnected characters in this play, which—inspired by the artist Robert Rauschenberg—takes the form of a collage of scenes, images and texts. Bob's Mom weaves in and out, sharing with the audience stories of her son's youth—almost all of them ending with the same thought: "Art was not a part of our lives." In this speech, she talks about her grandmother.

BOB'S MOM: When I was sixteen my grandmother had to be put into a home. My grandmother had terrorized my mother and uncle for so many years it was difficult to feel much in the way of empathy or compassion or love for her. But I related to her in one way. We shared a real passion for the color red. My grandmother's house was a museum. She collected cut Italian colored glass decanters and glasses. Each object was uniquely shaped. Colors rich. I valued those objects deeply. I wanted to play with them, to make new shapes of them, to make new surfaces for them. I wanted to smash them and see what they looked like as heaps, to see how light played on their shattered surfaces. My grandmother always wore a large, rectangular, ruby pendant on a gold chain. I dreamed of having that one day. Of having that color. When my grandmother died I asked what became of the ruby. It turned out she had gone into the home years before and everything was sold at a yard sale. The objects she collected—beautiful objects—all discarded. Thrown out. No one wanted them. Cast off. I would have preferred to smash them against brick walls to see what they might have become.

Well, art was not a part of our lives.

SEARCH AND DESTROY

By Howard Korder

Marie, an ambitious receptionist, has written the script for a horror movie. Over dinner in an airport snack bar, she pitches it to a film producer.

MARIE: Everybody's dead all over. Okay. She's caught. The spinesucker has her pinned against the wall. With his other hand he cracks open her boyfriend's head and smears his brains all over her tits. Okay. The elevator's stuck between floors. This thing comes out of him like a gangrene penis with a lobster claw and starts burrowing into her. The pain's unbearable. Okay. Finally she manages to reach the switch on the radial saw and rips it into him. But he just smiles, okay, his stomach opens up and he absorbs it, like he does and goes on pumping her up. She's gonna die, that's all. *Except* inside him the saw's still going, spinning around, he starts shaking and there's a, what do you, close shot, yeah, and the saw rips out of his chest, there's this explosion of meat and pus pouring out like from a fire hose, he climbs on her and tries to shove the penis claw down her throat, okay, but she hacks it off with the saw okay he goes shooting back against the glass door okay they break he falls five floors, onto the metal spike in the fountain it goes straight through his face, his brains spurt out and slide into the water like fresh come okay. He's dead, he's dead, he's finally fucking dead. She walks away that's the end.

THE GIMMICK

By Dael Orlandersmith

Dael Orlandersmith's The Gimmick *grew out of a conversation with director Peter Askin about the world of children, the author explains in an* American Theatre *interview. "He asked something about how kids from similar backgrounds, similarly difficult environments, fare so differently" —how some beat the odds and others don't. Orlandersmith turned the idea into a full-length monologue about childhood friends Alexis and Jimmy, a writer and an artist, and the divergent paths they take as they move into adulthood. Here, Alexis remembers when they were children and first became friends.*

ALEXIS: . . . me and Jimmy go to my room and he shows me pictures he's painted / lots of pictures / all over the room / there are pictures of Superman / Superman with captions / DRUGS CAN KILL / Superman living in Mount Morris Park killing drug dealers / pictures of Superman being friends with a small black boy / SUPERMAN'S BEST FRIEND JIMMY / "He talks to me, Superman does / 'Jimmy, I will fight all crime / I will let no one hurt you / you're my friend / you and all children' / I tell people he talks to me / they say I'm lying / but I don't care / he talks to me in a secret language / nobody else can understand / I paint Superman 'cause he's good / see how he can fly, Alexis / he can fly / nobody can touch him / he can fly."

"What do you like to play, huh, Alexis? / What do you like to do?" / I show him a notebook with a story / I'm scared / but I give it to him / my notebook / "You can read it," I say / outside I say, "You can read it" / inside I say, Don't laugh at me / outside I say, "I'm going to be a famous writer one day" / inside I say, Don't laugh at me / don't tell the other kids on the block / outside I say, "I write a lot even though I'm eight years old / I like to write / I'm not like these stupid kids around here" / inside I say, The other kids don't like me / they laugh at me / Be my friend you read my story and be my friend.

He looks at my notebook / frowns / looks and frowns / shakes his head / Inside I say, He's laughing at me, laughing at me, I'll beat his ass / jack him up for laughing at me / outside I say, "Gimme it back / you don't like it / gimme it back" / and I snatch my book / "No / no, Alexis, I ain't good with words" / "I don't understand" / "Me neither"/ But he didn't laugh at me / he was my friend / he didn't laugh / and I read the story to him.

I read about a girl / a fat girl who lives in a dirty house / then wakes up thin in a clean house / and Jimmy says, "That girl, that's you, right? / Alexis / that girl is you, right / I can tell that's you" / But I say, "It's my friend / it's not me / I know someone / it's not me" / Jimmy looks long / hard / deep / "No / not no friend / it's you Alexis / it's you."

Later we go to Jimmy's house / his house a motherless house / we're watching *American Bandstand* [. . .] Jimmy and me didn't know / didn't see black or white / we were kids / we saw / but we didn't see / We didn't understand why we couldn't live like *American Bandstand* kids on TV / Me and Jimmy / we prick our fingers / mix blood and say / I love you love me / forever and ever / you and me.

THE GIMMICK

By Dael Orlandersmith

This speech picks up Alexis and Jimmy's story some years later.
     Note: Clarence is Jimmy's father, Lenny is Alexis's mother; both are alcoholics.

ALEXIS: The next week Jimmy brings me to his teacher's studio / Mr. Kaufman's studio / He smiles a slow smile, talks in a cool voice / a voice trying to be cool because he's really excited / "I have the key / Mr. Kaufman gave me the key / says I can paint here whenever I want / Mr. K / he's cool / he's cool / And know what else he said, Alexis? / He said, 'Jimmy / you have something special to give the world / so special' / I want to be / I want to be so bad, Alexis / so bad / If I could be great, Alexis" / He stops / looks around at Mr. Kaufman's studio / then in a whisper / more like a whisper / says, "God, Alexis / God / Maybe there is one / a God / huh, Alexis? / Maybe there is one / I feel so good, man" / He spins and grins / spins / grins / stops / "Maybe I can't, Alexis / Maybe I don't deserve to do good" / And I say, "Naw man, hush, hush / cut that / cut that / Jimmy" / "Damn, Alexis," he lights a joint / I say, "Naw, naw Jimmy you don't need it / It's good with Mr. Kaufman / you don't need to do that / No, you're great, trust me / heart to heart."

Jimmy paints / paints angry pieces / frightened black boys / frightened black girls / crying black boys / crying black girls / Harlem's Munch / There's one piece / one / a black boy / a black boy in a chair with colors / colors of Orange / Red / Black 'n' Blue / This boy sits in a chair by a kitchen window in Harlem / looking through locked bars onto an empty street / The boy's eyes are wide / sad / "Know what I call that piece / I call it *Solo* / that's the name of it, man / *Solo*."

It was the color spectrum of pain / Pain in total color / slashes of light / color / Jimmy Knew it from Clarence / I knew it from Lenny / How each slap / punch was a spectrum of Orange / Red / Black / Blue.

Jimmy paints and drinks / I say to Jimmy, "Don't do that / don't be like Clarence and Lenny / You'll end up like them" / "No, no, no, Alexis, not like them / So I don't have to feel bad anymore / so I don't have to feel."

One day I say to Jimmy, "Let's make the colors happy colors / not just hurt colors / Let's make them happy" / "What do you mean, Alexis?" / I say, "Not just orange red blood, Jimmy / Think of something good with orange red" / "I can only think of blood, Alexis" / "But blood keeps you alive, Jimmy / Think about when we go to Paris / Blood keeps you alive" / "Red orange blood is life / not just pain / it's life" / And I say, "Yeah, Jimmy / life."

I'd watch him and he'd paint me / I'd let him paint me / He'd paint me heavy-boned / heavy-eyelidded, like Picasso's women / He'd paint my hands, large expressive / my shoulders / sloping / big / fine-boned / He'd see the browns and yellows of my shoulders and I say, "You should paint my breast too, Jimmy" / His eyes get big / "Yeah, okay / you sure?" / "Yeah, I'm sure" / I remove my shirt / It was strange / in Jimmy's room / It was still / quiet / still and strange.

Then it got fine / real fine / "You're doing it, Jimmy, just like Picasso" / We're gonna go Jimmy / We're gonna go to Paris / We'll meet twice a week / you paint me / I'll write / We'll go / When we're eighteen we'll go.

Now Jimmy really begins to paint me / Before it was pencils / crayons / sketches / now he is totally on canvas / painting me on canvas like Picasso's women / heavy-boned / heavy-eyelidded / Jimmy glows / "This is for you, Alexis / do you like it? / Man I hope you like it / couldn't have done it without you / you my muse / you my muse, Alexis, girl" / Glowing / glowing / he gives me my portrait / a swirl of colors / not just Orange / Red / Black 'n' Blue / My portrait was gold / I saw gold / I was gold / "Now everybody can see it, Alexis / How beautiful you are" / Jimmy made me look / strong, beautiful / Perhaps Jimmy saw those things because those things were in him / strength / beauty / but he didn't know it / He didn't know he was filled with so many colors / not just hurt ones / many ones / We set a time twice a week / I'd sit before him naked / "Big is more better / Notice how Picasso makes his girls big, Alexis?" / And I'd write and read my words in broad strokes / He broad stroked with paint / I with language / I'd create color with language / And the world was endless / Endless strokes of paint / Endless words on paper / How endless the world was.

10
"THERE'S BAD BLOOD BETWEEN US . . ."

THE MINEOLA TWINS

By Paula Vogel

Paula Vogel describes this play as "a comedy in seven scenes, four dreams and five wigs" in which "all of the characters should be played in a constant state of high hormonal excitement." It traces some four decades in the lives of two twins— Myrna, "the good twin" (who saved herself for marriage and grew up to be a right-winger) and Myra, "the evil twin" (who slept with Myrna's high school boyfriend—not to mention their school's football team—and grew up to be an anti-war activist). This speech (Dream Sequence Number Two: "Myrna in the Hospital. Myrna in Hell.") takes place when Myrna is in a psychiatric hospital. It is Myrna's fantasy of killing her sister.

Note: Kenny is Myrna's son. Words in the script which appear in boldface are the voice that the sisters hear in their dreams.

MYRNA: So. I will be dressed in my London Fog raincoat, with my Coach bag accessories, neatly coiffed, because Dr. Prior says hygiene is a sign of mental health.

I'll park behind the trailer, next to the dump right off Jericho Turnpike. Then I'll knock at her screen door. My sister will answer the door, still drowsy from her night shift. But she'll pretend not to be surprised. "Can I come in?" I'll ask. She turns and leaves the screen door open. I enter. It's a pigsty; high heels are dropped willy-nilly; dirty dishes pile in the sink. A trail of socks leads to the platform bed in the back. She sits down at the table and waits. "Listen—" I say: "Can we have a cup of tea together?"

As she makes the tea, I chatter. She searches for a clean cup. It's not very. She pours the water. She dumps the cups on the table and the water sloshes over the rim of my cup. You'd swear she was never a waitress—"Oh—Myra," I say—"You've left the stove on!"

As my sister turns, swiftly I take the vial from my pocket and pour it into her cup. Then I quickly add two sugars and stir as she turns back— "You do take sugar, don't you?" She does. I don't. I never have. We sip our tea.

"There's bad blood between us, Myra. I want to clear up the bad blood."

Myra nods. Her head continues to nod in slower and slower circles. I catch the teacup before it falls, the drug already coursing through her blood. Quickly I go to work. I put on my Playtex Living Gloves, my rain bonnet and my London Fog. I carefully wash her cup, and put it away. Then I open Myra's old diary that I filched from Mom and Daddy's House. I open it to the incident with the football captain. I put the suicide note on the table with the handwriting that looks just like hers, the letter trailing off after: "I Can't Go On This Way . . ."

Then I open the trunk of my car and take out Daddy's Hunting Rifle. I giggle, because I've never held anything more dangerous than a soup ladle. But I know just what to do. Kneeling beside my sister, I take off her right shoe. I toss it on the floor. I take off her right sock—I just toss it. Then I brace the rifle at a jaunty angle so that her big toe jams the trigger while her mouth sucks the double barrel—just like old times with the football team.

I turn up her record player. Jazz pours out; I crank up the volume. Then I kneel beside her and whisper: "This is real, you asshole, this is happening." For the first time in years, my sister and I touch as I press her big toe on the trigger. We squeeze the trigger together. It sounds like *champagne*. I don't want to look. I expect to see hamburger, ground chuck at forty-nine cents a pound. But from the stem of her neck, where her head used to be—there's a bouquet. Her brains have flowered. *Les Fleurs du mal.* "It's so pretty, Myra!" I tell her. I touch a single stem. I'll take a flower home and press it in my diary. Maybe when he's old enough, I'll give it to Kenny.

Kenny. What am I going to tell little Kenny? *The truth.* Tell Kenny the truth. **Aunt Myra has gone on a long, long trip. Far across the border. And she's never coming back.**

BETTY'S SUMMER VACATION

By Christopher Durang

Mrs. Siezmagraff is, Christopher Durang writes, a vibrant, "Auntie Mame-ish" woman in her mid-forties who is oblivious to anyone else's discomfort—especially her daughter Trudy's. As a child, Trudy was molested by her father (something Mrs. Siezmagraff has cheerfully ignored for many years); now she has responded to a new trauma of Trudy's—being raped by Mr. Vanislaw (an insane derelict and sex addict her mother invited into their vacation home) and then killing and dismembering her attacker. In an American Theatre *interview, which the author conducted with himself, Durang acknowledges his exaggerated style of black comedy: "I think my sense of humor asks for a complicated response. I ask people to laugh at things that I know are serious and tragic." In this monologue (deemed "good practice for the real COURT TV trial"), Mrs. Siezmagraff starts out defending Trudy, and ends up being put on trial herself for the psychological abuse she has inflicted on her. It demands a tour-de-force performance.*

MRS. SIEZMAGRAFF *(As defense attorney)*: I call Mrs. Siezmagraff to the witness stand. *(Calls out, as if she's the bailiff now as well)* Mrs. Siezmagraff! Mrs. Siezmagraff! Come to the witness stand. *(Speaking as herself)* Coming! *(As bailiff, running the words together)* Do you swear to tell the truth, the whole truth and nothing but the truth? *(As herself)* I do. *(As defense attorney, interrogating)* Mrs. Siezmagraff, you are the mother of the accused, are you not? *(As herself)* Yes I am. *(As defense attorney)* May I say that you are looking especially lovely this evening? *(As herself, genuinely flattered)* Oh, thank you. [. . .]

(As attorney) Mrs. Siezmagraff, did you know that your husband, Trudy's father, raped her repeatedly in her childhood? *(As herself, angry; her eyes flash)* Did she tell you that? She's a liar! [. . .] I have to tell the truth, Trudy. *(As attorney)* Mrs. Siezmagraff, is it not true that Trudy told you what was happening, and you refused to believe her? *(As herself)* She never told me. She never told me anything. I was a perfect mother. I don't know why she's telling these lies about me! *(As attorney)* I call to the stand, Mrs. McGillicutty, your Irish housekeeper. *(As herself, baffled)* I never had a housekeeper. I don't know who you're talking about. *(As attorney)* Mrs. McGillicutty, you were in the employ of Mrs. Siezmagraff over there, were you not? *(Now she's the Irish maid, speaking with a very pronounced Irish accent)* Oh, b'gosh and b'garin, yes, I worked for Mrs. Siezmagraff for many years. *(As herself)* That's a lie! She's a liar! *(As attorney)* Be quiet! Mrs. McGillicutty, can you prove to us that you worked for Mrs. Siezmagraff? *(As Irish maid)* Oh yes, m'lord. Here are my pay stubs for my work for five years. *(As herself)* Those are forgeries! I've never seen this woman before in my life! *(As Irish maid)* B'gosh and b'garin, Mrs. Siezmagraff, don't you recognize me? I'm Kathleen. I come all the way from Kilarney to be with your family and mind your little daughter Trudy. *(As herself, getting hysterical)* I've never seen you. You're a liar. Listen to her accent. She's not really Irish. *(As Irish maid, offended)* I am Irish. And I worked for you for five years. Trudy remembers me, don't you, Trudy? [. . .]

(As herself) Trudy, you're lying! *(As attorney)* Don't be afraid of your mother, Trudy. Just tell the court the truth. *(As Irish maid)* Oh, Trudy. Remember you and I spent many a happy hour. I would read you stories about the leprechauns and the funny mischief they would do. You remember, don't you, Trudy? [. . .]

(As attorney) Mrs. McGillicutty. Did you ever see Trudy's father molest her. *(As Irish maid)* Yes, I did. *(As herself)* She's lying! *(As attorney)* And do you have any first-hand knowledge that Trudy's mother knew her husband was molesting Trudy? *(As Irish maid)* Yes, I do. *(As herself, vicious and seething)* That's not true! She's lying! *(As attorney)* Mrs. McGillicutty, what is the knowledge that you have? *(As Irish maid)* On April 4th, 1978, Mrs. Siezmagraff said to me, "I know my husband is raping my daughter, but I don't want to say anything to him, because I'm afraid he'd leave me." *(As herself)* You Irish pig! You liar! *(As Irish maid)* And when she said that, I happened to be speaking into a tape recorder, making a transcription of my special Irish stew recipe, and so I have a recording of her admission on tape. So don't you be calling me a liar, Mrs. Siezmagraff. I'll take you to court and sue you for slander.

(Mrs. Siezmagraff, caught by the Irish maid's evidence, now has full-fledged hysterics, and rushes center stage) It's true! It's true! I knew what was going on. And I didn't stop it. I was afraid I'd lose him. It's my fault Trudy was molested over and over and over, and no wonder she attacked Mr. Vanislaw. And I could've stopped Mr. Vanislaw's raping her, but I was drunk! I had had seven margaritas and I passed out. *(Weeps)* I'm sorry, Trudy, I'm sorry—I ruined your life. *(Crescendo—on her knees, out front)* Don't convict my daughter! It's my fault. I didn't protect her. It's my fault. Convict me, convict me! *(Collapses to the ground, weeps)*

THREE DAYS OF RAIN

By Richard Greenberg

Nan, a mother of two now living in Boston, has returned to Manhattan for the reading of her father's will. He was a famous architect; Nan's mother was "sort of like Zelda Fitzgerald's less-stable sister." The reading of the will is also cause for a tenuous reunion between Nan and her brother Walker, who she hasn't seen since he disappeared a year earlier. Here, Nan (speaking alternately with Walker in a double soliloquy) tells the audience what she believes her parents' lives were like when they first met, and describes one terrible day some years after they married when her mother "flew out the apartment and down the thousands of flights of stairs to the lobby."

NAN: My parents married because it was 1960 and one had to and they were there. And I don't think that's a contemptible thing—for people who have reached a certain age and never found anything better. I mean, forget about what happened later, think of the *moment*. My mother was lovely, but not as young as she should have been, my father was virtually silent, and they *found* each other and I don't think that's so cynical. He was presentable and serious and he must have seemed calming to her, and solid, and easy to ignore, but not in a bad way. And he was from New England and later New York, so he probably thought she wasn't crazy, just Southern. And if it was calculating, it was a calculation against loneliness, against . . . the possibility of no life at all.

    On May 12th, 1972, at around eight P.M., I was in the kitchen of our eleven-room apartment on the Upper East Side, finishing up the dishes and humming. We were living then in a terrible skyscraper my father had designed, his first skyscraper— [. . .] My brother, who was eight, was in his pajamas, on the living room floor, erecting cities out of this super-sophisticated Tinker Toy kind of thing my father had made for us. My father sat in a large, uncomfortable Modern chair, flipping silently through a large art book— [. . .] I had done the dishes and was moving onto the water glasses when something happened. The first indication I had was the sound of my brother laughing. He later told me he hadn't reacted to anything new, he'd just looked up and in an instant really seen what was happening— [. . .] My brother pursued her but couldn't catch her— [. . .] He did arrive in time however to see her body pierce the glass façade of the building— [. . .] My brother was eight years old.

Meanwhile, upstairs, my father, acting on a hunch, instructed me to telephone for an ambulance while he joined them in the chase. I called the ambulance, dried the glasses from dinner, and sat on the long, steep, uncomfortable couch. Waiting. I was ten.

Sometimes, I ask people, "So how did all of this happen?" and they say, "Oh, well, your poor mother, you know, and then, it *was* the sixties." At any rate. My mother was taken to the hospital where they did very good work. My brother ran away, but only as far as the laundry room of our building, where he hid in a closet for ten hours until someone thought to check there. My brother returned, my mother returned. Nobody said anything. And it was over.

11

"THE ONES WHO CROSSED THE OCEAN . . ."

ANGELS IN AMERICA, PART ONE: MILLENNIUM APPROACHES

By Tony Kushner

Rabbi Isidor Chemelwitz is the orthodox Jewish rabbi whose only speech, a eulogy delivered at the funeral for the grand-mother of the character Louis Ironson, begins the play. He speaks with a heavy Eastern European accent, consulting a sheet of notes. In Kushner's sprawling "gay fantasia on national themes," the character is written to be played by a woman, the actor who also plays the role of Hannah Pitt (a Mormon from Salt lake City, who is visiting her son in New York).

RABBI ISIDOR CHEMELWITZ: Hello and good morning. I am Rabbi Isidor Chemelwitz of the Bronx Home for Aged Hebrews. We are here this morning to pay respects at the pass-ing of Sarah Ironson, devoted wife of Benjamin Ironson, also deceased, loving and caring mother of her sons Morris, Abra-ham, and Samuel, and her daughters Esther and Rachel; beloved grandmother of Max, Mark, Louis, Lisa, Maria . . . uh . . . Lesley, Angela, Luke, and Eric. Eric? This is a Jewish name? *(Shrugs)* Eric. A large and loving family. We assemble that we may mourn collectively this good and righteous woman.

This woman. I did not know this woman. I cannot accu-rately describe her attributes, nor do justice to her dimensions. She was . . . Well, in the Bronx Home of Aged Hebrews are many like this, the old, and to many I speak but not to be frank with this one. She preferred silence. So I do not know her and yet I know her. We are all the same, of this generation. We are the last of our kind.

In her was—not a person but a whole kind of person— the ones who crossed the ocean, who brought with us to America the villages of Russia and Lithuania—and how we struggled, and how we fought, for the family, for the Jewish home, so that you would not grow up *here*, in this strange place, in the melting pot where nothing melted. Descendants of this immigrant woman, you do not grow up in America, you and your children and their children with the goyische names, you do not live in America, no such place exists, your clay is the clay of some Litvak shtetl, your air the air of the steppes—because she carried the old world on her back across the ocean, in a boat, and she put it down on Grand Concourse Avenue, or in Flatbush, and she worked that earth into your bones, and you pass it to your children, this ancient, ancient culture and home.

(Little pause)

You can never make that crossing that she made, for such Great Voyages in this world do not any more exist. But every day of your lives the miles that voyage between that place and this one you cross. Every day. You understand me? In you that journey is.

So . . .

She was the last of the Mohicans, this one was. Pretty soon . . . all the old will be dead.

TONGUE OF A BIRD

By Ellen McLaughlin

Zofia, an old woman, lives alone in a dust-filled house in the mountains. Her granddaughter, Maxine, has recently arrived bearing a laundry bag (holding nearly all of her earthly pos-

sessions) and a slice of cake, which prompts Zofia's memory of when she first arrived in America.

ZOFIA: It was the strangest thing. All the children who arrived in New York off the first boat from Poland. Some rich woman sent cake to us, chocolate cake. And we stood on the dock and ate it. It was the first thing I tasted in America. Some . . . what-do-you-call—eccentric millionaire woman, I forget her name, she sends all the children of the war cake. After that our troubles began. But at that time I thought, so this is what it will always be like here. Chocolate cake and the salt air, and the sugar frosting on my wool gloves. [. . .] Someone had thought of us. [. . .]

It's good. [. . .] That you can put your whole life into a . . . everything you can hold into a . . . *(She can't find the word, she snaps her fingers with impatience)* No, not "laundry," not "bag" . . . Ach, "*torebka*" . . . [. . .] Sak! Sak, sak, sak! Yes. That you can do that, you learned from me that. Yes. Good. [. . .] Oh, yes. All you need you have to carry here. *(She taps her head)* Because everything else they can take from you. [. . .] Who takes? *(She laughs)* The world. *(She gestures out)* That. *(She taps her head)* This is all you can take. When I was a little girl, walking out of Poland after the bombs . . . the ones of us who were left. Ach. We took all the wrong things . . . little spoons, a duck, a purple table runner . . . We were so stupid. We would be holding all the wrong things for the rest of our lives, no matter where we went . . . Ach. I would hold the little comb to my chest all night long on the boat across the ocean, because I cannot hold my mother's hand, never again. And I think, this will save me. This will be enough. A comb she gave me. Because her hand had been on it. This will save me. This thing. [. . .] I threw it in the ocean. It was not enough. The cup my dead father made for me, her glove . . . seven silver buttons . . . *(She makes a gesture of throwing)* I walked off that boat with nothing in my hands. Like an animal. I made myself do that. Skin and bones and this. *(She touches her head)*

HUNTING COCKROACHES

By Janusz Glowacki

Anka, a Polish immigrant now living in New York, introduces herself to the audience. She lives with her husband, Janek, in a squalid, cockroach-infested room that is simultaneously living room, bedroom and kitchen. A huge map of America, to which Anka makes reference in this speech, hangs on the wall.

ANKA: My name is Anka. I can't sleep. I'm a nervous wreck. I'm Polish. I've been in New York for three years. For the past three months I can't get any sleep. I mean, at first I couldn't sleep for something like a month, then I could, and then I couldn't and then I could again. Now for the past forty-two days—or maybe it's twenty-two days—I can't sleep at all. *(Studying the audience)* I'm an actress . . . I can't get any parts due to my accent. They say I have an awful accent . . . do I? That's my husband, Janek . . . *(Points to him)* He can't sleep either. He's just pretending he's asleep . . . *(Smiles)* I know it. He can't fall asleep without his pills and I hid them. *(Looks around, pulls a bottle of pills from under the mattress, and shows them to the audience)* See! *(Smiles triumphantly)* To tell the truth the pills don't help him any, but he loves searching for them. He's a writer . . . He was very famous in Poland . . . a novel of his came out in Paris . . . One of his plays was produced in New York. *(Looks around the audience)* His name is Krupinski, Jan Krupinski. *(Pauses for a moment; spells it out)* K-R-U-P-I-N-S-K-I . . . Never heard of him? It's a good thing he's asleep. I mean, he's pretending . . . Look, I've got a whole bunch of reviews. He got a very good one in the *New York Times*, and a real bad one in the *Village Voice*. I got an award for my interpretation of Lady Macbeth in Warsaw. I know it's completely moronic but here in America you have to praise yourself, right? If you don't have any confidence in yourself, who's going to. Do I really have an awful accent? I did some work for an art critic from Poland who's well connected, he worked in an Italian restaurant at Second Avenue and 88th Street. He got me a temporary job at the Museum of Immigration. I'd appear every noon dressed as a nineteenth-century Polish immigrant. *(Ironically)* You know the outfit . . . babushka, boots. But now the museum is being repaired . . . *(Throws up her hands as if to say, "What can I do?")* Isn't he good at pretending he's asleep. I taught him how. If it gets out he can't sleep, we're finished. In New York everybody knows how to sleep. I'm trying to get him to pretend he's happy. In New York everybody's happy. In the daytime he usually sits in front of the map. *(Points to the map hanging on the wall. She gets up and goes over to the map, sits down in front of it. Looks at the map for a while in silence)* He can sit like this for an hour or two. *(Again she looks at the map in silence)* Then he says: "What a strange country!" That's all. "What a strange country!" I told him he'd never make it here because he doesn't have a sincere smile. Everybody here has a sincere smile. In Eastern Europe nobody has a sincere smile, except drunks and informers. *(Smiles)* Yesterday he sat in front of the map and practiced the art of the sincere smile, checking it every so often in the mirror. I told him he should write a play about Polish émigrés, but he said the subject is boring, either you make it or you don't.

12

"YES, YOU ARE, HE SAID; *YOU'RE* THAT KIND OF GIRL."

THREE TALL WOMEN

By Edward Albee

The "three tall women" of Edward Albee's Pulitzer Prize–winning play are, it is revealed to the audience in the second act, one woman captured at three different times in her life. C is the youngest. All of her dreams—and her disappointments—are still in the future. At twenty-six, she wears lovely frocks and twirls and sashays. She tells her older selves, B and A, about her "first time."

C: I'm a good girl. I know how to attract *men*. I'm *tall*; I'm striking; *I* know how to do it. Sis slouches and caves her front in; I stand tall, breasts out, chin up, hands . . . just so. I walk between the aisles and they know there's somebody coming, that there's somebody *there*. But, I'm a *good girl*. I'm not a virgin, but I'm a good girl. The boy who took me was a good boy.

(C does not necessarily hear—or, at least, notice—the asides to come.)

> [B: Oh, yes he *was*.
> A: Yes? Was he?
> B: *You* remember.
> A *(Laughs)*: Well, it *was* a *while* ago.
> B: But you *do* remember.
> A: Oh, yes. I remember him. He was . . .]

C: . . . sweet and handsome; no, not handsome: beautiful: he was beautiful!

> [A *(To B)*: He was; yes.
> B *(To A and herself)*: Yes.]

C: He has coal-black hair and violet eyes and such a smile!

> [A: Ah!
> B: Yes!]

C: His body was . . . well, it was thin, but *hard*; all sinew and muscle; he fenced, he told me, and he was the one with the megaphone on the crew. When I held him when we danced, there was only sinew and muscle. We dated a lot; I liked him; I didn't tell Mother, but I liked him a lot. I like him, Sis, I said; I really like him. Have you told Mother? No, and don't *you*; I like him a lot, but I don't *know*. Has he . . . *you* know. No, I said; no, he hasn't. But then he did. We were dancing—slowly—late, at the end of the evening, and we danced so close, all . . . pressed, and . . . we were pressed, and I could feel that he was hard, *that* muscle and sinew, pressed against me while we danced. We were the same height and he looked into my eyes as we danced, slowly, and I felt the pressure up against me, and he tensed it and I felt it move against me.

> [B *(Dreamy)*: Whatever is *that*, I said.
> A: Hmmmmmmmmm.]

C: Whatever is *that*, I said. I *knew*, but whatever is that, I said, and he smiled, and his eyes shone, and it's me in love with you, he said. You have an interesting way of showing it, I said. Appropriate, he said, and I felt the muscle move again, and . . . well, I knew it was time; I knew I was ready, and I knew I wanted him—whatever that *meant*—that I wanted *him*, that I wanted *it*.

[B *(Looking back; agreeing)*: Yes; oh, yes.
A: Hmmmmmmmm.]

C: Remember, don't give it away, Mother said; don't give it away like it was nothing.

[B *(Remembering)*: They won't respect you for it and you'll get known as a loose girl. *Then* who will you marry?
A *(To B)*: Is that what she said? I can't remember.
B *(Laughs)*: *Yes* you can.]

C: They won't respect you for it and you'll get known as a loose girl. *Then* who will you marry? But he was pressed against me, exactly where he wanted to be—we were the same height—and he was *so* beautiful, and his eyes shone, and he smiled at me and he moved his hips as we danced, so slowly, as we danced, and he breathed on my neck and he said, you don't want me to embarrass myself right here on the dance floor, do you?

[B *(Remembering)*: No, no; of course not.]

C: I said, no, no; of course not. Let's go to my place, he said, and I heard myself saying *(Incredulous)* I'm not that kind of girl? I mean, as soon as I said it, I blushed: it was so . . . stupid, so . . . expected. Yes, you are, he said; *you're* that kind of girl.

[B: And I was, and my God it was wonderful.
A: It hurt! *(Afterthought; to B)* Didn't it?
B *(Admonishing)*: Oh . . . well, a little.]

C: You're that kind of girl, and I guess I was.

PICASSO AT THE LAPIN AGILE

By Steve Martin

In 1904, when Steve Martin's comedy takes place, Pablo Picasso is twenty-three and not yet famous. Suzanne is nineteen. In this speech, she tells the story of how they met. Suzanne hasn't seen Picasso since the events described here, but she knows that he's the kind of person who inspires others to "either want to run like hell or go with it." She is going with it.

SUZANNE: I . . . it was about two weeks ago. I was walking down the street one afternoon and I turned up the stairs into my flat and I looked back and he was there framed in the doorway looking up at me. I couldn't see his face because the light came in from behind him and he was in shadow and he said, "I am Picasso." And I said, "Well so what?" And then he said he wasn't sure yet but he thinks that it means something in the future to be Picasso. He said that occasionally there is a Picasso and he happens to be him but that was okay. He said the twentieth century has to start somewhere and why not now. Then he said may I approach you and I said okay. He walked upstairs and picked up my wrist and turned it over and took his fingernail and scratched deeply on the back of my hand. In a second, in red, the image of a dove appeared. Then I thought, why is it that some guy who wants me can hang around for months, and I even like the guy but I'm not going to sleep with him, but some other guy says the right thing and I'm on my back, not knowing what hit me. [. . .]

See, men are always talking about their things. Like it's not them. [. . .] The things between their legs. [. . .] See! It's not them; it's someone else. And it's true; it's like some rudderless firework snaking across town. But women have things too, they just work differently. They work from up here. *(She taps her head)* So when the guy comes on to me through up here, he's practically there already, done. So the next thing I know he's inside the apartment and I said what do you want and he said he wanted my hair, he wanted my neck, my knees, my feet. He wanted his eyes on my eyes, his chest on my chest. He wanted the chairs in the room, the notepaper on the table; he wanted the paint off the walls. He wanted to consume me until there was nothing left. He said he wanted deliverance, and that I would be his savior. And he was speaking Spanish, which didn't hurt I'll tell you. Well at that point, the word "no" became like a Polish village: unpronounceable.

ROOSTERS

By Milcha Sanchez-Scott

The American Southwest. Chata, a tough, cigarette-smoking woman of forty, "gives new meaning to the word blowsy. She has the lumpy face of a hard boozer . . . She wears a black kimono, on the back of which is embroidered in red a dragon and the words 'Korea, U.S.S. Perkins, 7th Fleet.'" She explains to her sister-in-law the relationship between making tortillas and being a woman.

CHATA: Ah, you people don't know what it is to eat fresh handmade tortillas. My grandmother Hortensia, the one they used to call "La India Condenada" . . . she would start making them at five o'clock in the morning. So the men would have something to eat when they went into the fields. Hijo! She was tough . . . Use to break her own horses . . . and her own men. Every day at five o'clock she would wake me up. "Buenos pinchi días," she would say. I was twelve or thirteen years old, still in braids . . . "Press your hands into the dough," "Con fuerza," "Put your stamp on it." One day I woke up, tú sabes, con la sangre. "Ah! So you're a woman now. Got your own cycle like the moon. Soon you'll want a man, well this is what you do. When you see the one you want, you roll the tortilla on the inside of your thigh and then you give it to him nice and warm. Be sure you give it to him and nobody else." Well, I been rolling tortillas on my thighs, on my nalgas, and God only knows where else, but I've been giving my tortillas to the wrong men . . . and that's been the problem with my life. First there was Emilio. I gave him my first tortilla. Ay Mamacita, he use to say, these are delicious. Aye, he was handsome, a real lady-killer! After he did me the favor he didn't even have the cojones to stick around . . . took my TV set too.

13

"AREN'T HUMAN BEINGS THE SADDEST PEOPLE YOU EVER MET?"

THE SWAN

By Elizabeth Egloff

Dora, a nurse, hasn't had much luck with her relationships. She's been through a series of failed marriages, and her current lover won't leave his wife. When she is woken from an exhausted sleep by an enormous swan that has crashed into her plate-glass window, Dora reacts first with fear, then with equanimity after the swan is transformed into a naked man. In Egloff's partly realistic, partly fantastical play, Dora and the swan, whom she names Bill, begin a romantic relationship. In the following two speeches, she confides in him about the men in her life that she has loved and lost.

DORA: Clothes, on the other hand, are very important. Duane, the first time I met Duane, he was wearing a French suit, Italian shoes and a Brazilian crocodile coat. Duane had more clothes than anybody I ever met. Then he got a job on an oil rig, and asked me to marry him. I'll never forget the day I waved him off at the pier. I was wearing a red tulle dress, six-inch yellow heels and a little white pillbox hat. I couldn't stop crying for a month. [. . .]

Another thing is music. Cheery music can make any of us feel cheerier. Some people don't realize this, as a result of which they go through life feeling something is terribly wrong if only they could put their finger on it. However. Working in a hospital taught me how to pick the right music. [. . .]

You ever been married, Bill? [. . .] I am a great supporter of marriage. I don't think people are meant to be alone. I don't think I am. Strange things happen to me when I'm alone. Dangerous things. [. . .] Like once I was in bed smoking a cigarette. And I'm lying there and I look up and I see a man standing in the door. He just walked into the house. He just opened the door and walked right into my house . . . And he's covered with leaves and there's grass in his hair and mud on his shoes. And he looks so sad and he looks so much like Gerry only that was before I'd ever met Gerry so how could he BUT there's something about him there's something in him that's warm that's comfortable someplace I could ease my aching heart and God! Aren't human beings the saddest people you ever met? And I looked at this guy, I looked at this total stranger and I thought yes you're right love is the only thing that matters if only I could get me some I could laugh again I could eat again I could belong to the world again, and just as I'm about to say yes, you're him you're the one, my cigarette is burning my fingers and I turn to put it out, and by the time I look back, he's gone. Disappeared. Evanesced. [. . .] I never saw him again. It's always the way, isn't it? Some people say I shouldn't marry so many, but I have to. They keep disappearing on me.

THE SWAN

By Elizabeth Egloff

DORA: Franklin always said, he said, Dora if you can't love yourself, then you can't love anyone. I said, but Franklin . . . I love you . . . Franklin was much too delicate for someone of my affections. If he hadn't left, I probably would have destroyed him altogether.

I don't think men are born on this planet. I think men are born on the planet Pluto and they have them molecularly disassembled and radared to the earth. Which is why. Which is why they are so, so, you have to take care of them in a very special way because they are foreign bodies being introduced to the system. And which is both why I love them and why I don't understand them whatever they're talking about.

I remember I met Gerry, you would think it was the day after he'd been radared to the earth. There was something about Gerry. Something tender, something baby, like here was a man who needed more time to adapt to the eco-system. Gerry was always talking to himself: What is love and why do we do it? The day after we got married he went out in the woods and shot himself. The whole thing didn't exactly inspire my confidence.

Duane inspired my confidence, or what was left of it. Duane breathed life into a millimeter of myself, the piece of shrapnel I have come to regard as my heart. I took one look at Duane and said, here's a man he doesn't ask questions, and he doesn't own a gun. Perfect, I thought, how could I go wrong? So I told him I loved him, and I loved myself. Duane said, how can you love yourself, if you don't love the world? Love the world, I said? I can hardly get out of bed. *(Beat)* Two days later, he ran off. I was joking.

ANGELS IN AMERICA, PART ONE: MILLENNIUM APPROACHES

By Tony Kushner

Harper Pitt describes herself as "a mentally deranged sex-starved pill-popping housewife." As another character puts it more succinctly, she is "amazingly unhappy." An agoraphobic Mormon with a mild Valium addiction and an obsession with the ozone layer, Harper is married to Joe, a closeted homo-sexual—something both characters secretly know, although neither of them will allow themselves to admit it. They have moved to Brooklyn from Salt Lake City so Joe could take a job in the Hall of Justice. This is Harper's first scene in the play. She begins by talking to the audience; midway through her speech she is joined by her imaginary friend Mr. Lies, a travel agent of the "International Order of Travel Agents," who tells her, "We mobilize the globe, we set people adrift, we stir the populace and send nomads eddying across the planet. We are adepts of motion, acolytes of the flux. Cash, check or credit card. Name your destination."

HARPER: People who are lonely, people left alone, sit talking nonsense to the air, imagining . . . beautiful systems dying, old fixed orders spiraling apart . . .

When you look at the ozone layer, from outside, from a spaceship, it looks like a pale blue halo, a gentle, shimmering aureole encircling the atmosphere encircling the earth. Thirty miles above our heads, a thin layer of three-atom oxygen molecules, product of photosynthesis, which explains the fussy vegetable preferences for visible light, its rejection of darker rays and emanations. Danger from without. It's a kind of gift, from God, the crowning touch to the creation of the world: guardian angels, hands linked, make a spherical net, a blue-green nesting orb, a shell of safety for life itself. But everywhere, things are collapsing, lies surfacing, systems of defense giving way . . . This is why, Joe, this is why I shouldn't be left alone.

(Little pause) I'd like to go traveling. Leave you behind to worry. I'll send postcards with strange stamps and tantalizing messages on the back. "Later maybe." "Nevermore."

(Mr. Lies, a travel agent, appears.)

Oh! You startled me! [. . .] I remember you. You're from Salt Lake. You sold us the plane tickets when we flew here. What are you doing in Brooklyn? [. . .]

I'm not safe here, you see. Things aren't right with me. Weird stuff happens . . . [. . .] Well, like you, for instance. Just appearing. Or last week . . . well never mind.

People are like planets, you need a thick skin. Things get to me. Joe stays away and now . . . Well look. My dreams are talking back to me. [. . .]

I'm undecided. I feel . . . that something's going to give. It's fifteen years till the second millennium. Maybe Christ will come again. Maybe seeds will be planted, maybe there'll be harvests then, maybe early figs to eat, maybe new life, maybe fresh blood, maybe companionship and love and protection, safety from what's outside, maybe the door will hold, or maybe . . . maybe the troubles will come, and the end will come, and the sky will collapse and there will be terrible rains and showers of poison light, or maybe my life is really fine, maybe Joe loves me and I'm only crazy thinking otherwise, or maybe not, maybe it's even worse than I know, maybe . . . I want to know, maybe I don't. The suspense, Mr. Lies, it's killing me.

THE CHEMISTRY OF CHANGE

By Marlane Meyer

Corlis lives with her glamorous, controlling mother and her brothers, including the charming and dissolute Baron, to whom she speaks here. Now thirty-nine and never married, Corlis remembers what happened long ago, when her mother, Lee, talked her out of eloping with her boyfriend Freddy. Corlis had her bags packed and Freddy was outside with a ladder against the window, when Lee pulled her back.

CORLIS: She said, he's not one of us, he's a creature. [. . .] She likened him to a worm that glows in the dark because he was losing his hair and he was so very self-conscious he smiled all the time and he had such big teeth. I just closed the window and turned off the light. I remember him crying. It was a windy night and I could hear him crying up to me. You went down and took him away and I never saw him again. He's made me hate the sound of wind and I used to love all nature. I saw in it this beautiful pattern of life, flowing, give and take, like the rising and falling of Freddy's breath when he would fall asleep reading to me. There was randomness and within it, human complement, Freddy and I, finding each other, in the bones of our bones, kindredness, destiny, coming right to our house delivering the mail . . . the male, see? The man, making me the woman . . . Now why is it I couldn't be the woman? [. . .] No, I'm not, because she couldn't believe that anyone would love me because I wasn't perfect. And she wouldn't let me love him because he wasn't perfect either. She made me feel ashamed to have loved him. Ashamed of loving. But now . . . I don't even know what I look like anymore. My female face and hands, breasts and legs, nobody has said anything about these things in such a long time, Baron.

MARVIN'S ROOM

By Scott McPherson

Bessie, age forty, lives with and takes care of her bedridden, stroke-impaired father, Marvin, and her Aunt Ruth, "a woman of seventy years with slight hunchback." Bessie herself has just been diagnosed with leukemia, leading to an uneasy family reunion with her estranged sister, Lee, and Lee's two sons, who have come home to be tested as possible bone marrow donors. Bessie surprises her sister by revealing that she once had a "true love," a boyfriend that no one in her family knew about, who ran the ferris wheel at the local carnival.

BESSIE: I knew he liked me because he always gave me an extra turn.

[LEE: That's sweet.]

BESSIE: Once he kept my car swaying at the top until I started to cry.

[LEE: He was a flirt.]

BESSIE: He had these big ears.

[LEE: I remember him. He was cute.]

BESSIE: He always said he probably came from England because of his name. Clarence James. He'd make a big deal out of his manners. He had the funniest laugh. He'd open his mouth real wide and no sound would come out.

[LEE: He was only there about three summers.]

BESSIE: Four summers.

[LEE: Then he stopped coming.]

BESSIE: That's right.

(Pause.)

[LEE: What happened?]

BESSIE: Nothing like you think.

[LEE: What happened?]

BESSIE: They always have a last picnic down by the river. This year there was kind of a cold snap, so a lot of people were bundled up. But Clarence—he'll deny it, but he likes to be the center of attention. Clarence goes swimming anyway. And he knows everybody is watching him. Everybody is there—his family, his friends, me. And he bobs up out of the water and he's laughing, making that monkey face, which gets all of us laughing, and he dunks under again and pops up somewhere else laughing even harder, which gets *us* laughing even harder. And he dives under again and then he doesn't come up and he doesn't come up and he doesn't come up. Laughing and choking looked the same on Clarence. He drowned right in front of us. Every time he came up for air, there we were chuckling and pointing. What could he have thought?

TALK RADIO

By Eric Bogosian

Linda MacArthur is the associate producer for Nighttalk, *Barry Champlain's talk-show radio program in Cleveland, Ohio. "Linda's job during the show is to make sure Barry has everything he needs, to keep track of when commercials are aired and generally to make sure the show is running smoothly,"* Bogosian writes in a stage direction. *"It is no coincidence that Linda is a very sexy blond." On his show, Barry is full of manic energy and self-assurance; he's got an edge. Speaking to the audience, Linda offers another view.*

LINDA: One night, after the show, I stopped by the lunch-room. I was thirsty, I was gonna get a Coke out of the machine. Barry was there. Sitting at the crummy table under the crummy fluorescent light. I didn't know him. I had been working here two months and he had said three words to me the whole time. He was sitting there staring at this ashtray full of butts. Just sitting. I asked him if anything was wrong . . . He looked up at me like he'd never seen me before. Like he didn't even know where he was. He said, "I'm outta cigarettes." I said, "There's a machine down the hall. I'll get you some." I mean, he coulda gotten the cigarettes himself, I know, but he seemed like he couldn't at that moment.

He looked at me again and said, "Linda, can I go home with you tonight? Can I sleep with you?" Now, I've had a lot of guys come on to me in a lot of ways. I expected this Barry guy to have a smooth approach but this was unexpectedly unique.

I didn't say yes. I didn't say no. We went to this diner he likes and I watched him eat a cheeseburger. He was talking about something, what was it? Euthanasia. I remember, because I thought this guy really knows how to sweet-talk a girl. And the whole time smoking cigarettes, looking around, tapping his fingers . . . Of course, we ended up at my place. As I was getting us drinks, I said to myself, "Linda you know you're gonna go to bed with this guy, so let's get the ball rolling." He was nervous, like he was going to jump out of his skin, so I started giving him a shoulder massage. The next thing, we're on the floor and he's kissing me like he was in the middle of the ocean, trying to get on a life raft!

I got us into the bedroom . . . and I go to the bathroom for two seconds to get myself together and anyway, when I get back to the bed, he's asleep, curled up in a ball.

All that night, while he slept, he's throwing himself around, tossing and turning, grinding his teeth, clenching his fists. It was scary. Next morning, he's up before me. Comes out of the shower, he's a different guy. Says he never slept so well. Then he comes over to the bed and . . . we made love . . .

Since then, we've spent maybe a dozen nights together . . . Lemme put it this way, Barry Champlain is a nice place to visit, but I wouldn't want to live there.

TALK RADIO

By Eric Bogosian

"You're pathetic," host Barry Champlain tells the callers to his late-night radio program, "I despise each and every one of you." Denise, in her only appearance, is one of the more fearful and paranoid.

DENISE: I'm scared Barry. [. . .] Nothing specifically, but on the other hand . . . you know, it's like everywhere I go . . . [. . .] Well, like, Barry, you know, like we've got a garbage disposal in our sink in the kitchen, I mean my mother's kitchen . . . [. . .] And sometimes a teaspoon will fall into the garbage disposal . . . [. . .] ya, so like you know how you feel when you have to reach down into that garbage disposal and you have to feel around down there for that teaspoon. You don't want to do it. Who knows what's down there? Could be garbage, a piece of something, so much stuff goes down there . . . or germs which you can't see. You can't see germs, but if they're gonna be anywhere, they're gonna be down that disposal. They grow there, see? They come back up the pipes. Salmonella, yeast, cancer, even the common cold, who knows? But, Barry, even without all that, what if, and I'm just saying "what if," 'cause it would probably never happen, but what if the garbage disposal came on while your hand is down there? [. . .] I get so scared of thinking about it that I usually leave the teaspoon there. I don't even try to get it out. But then I'm afraid that my mother will get mad if she finds it down there, so I turn the disposal on, trying to make it go down the drain. But all it does is make a huge racket. And I stand in the middle of the kitchen and the spoon goes around and around and I get sort of paralyzed, you know? It makes a lot of noise, incredible noise. But Barry, I kind of like that noise, because I know the teaspoon is getting destroyed and annihilated and that's good 'cause I hate the teaspoon for scaring me like that— [. . .]

Well it's not just the disposal, it's everything. What about insects? Termites. Hornets. Spiders. Ants. Centipedes. Mites. You can't even see the mites, they're like the germs. Tiny, impossible to see! I like things to be clean, you know. Dirty ashtrays bother me . . . just one more unknown. Just like the houses on our street. Used to be we knew who lived on our street. But that was years ago. Now all kinds of people live on our street. Even foreigners, people with accents. What are they doing on our street? What are their habits? Are they clean? Are they sanitary? [. . .] Oh sure, that would be a great idea just to go to somebody's house and just knock on the door. What if a serial murderer lived there? Ted Bundy? What if Ted Bundy or the Boston Strangler was just sitting inside watching television eating potato chips and I came to the door. Great! Come on in! [. . .] I don't go to strange people's houses. I keep the doors locked at all times. I stopped driving, but that isn't going to solve anything . . . You're not going to stop a plane from crashing into your house, now are you? [. . .]

The mailman brings me unsolicited mail and the postage stamp was licked by someone with AIDS. Right? My mother is a threat to my life just by persisting in going out there— [. . .] Do you know that there's this dust storm in California that has these little fungus spores in it? And these spores get in people's lungs and it goes into their bloodstreams and grows inside them and kills them? Strange air . . . strange air . . . you have to . . . Oh! there's my mother. I hear her key in the door. She'll kill me if she finds out I used the phone. *(Hang-up click)*

THE INCREDIBLY FAMOUS WILLY RIVERS

By Stephen Metcalfe

Willy Rivers is a rock star who becomes "incredibly famous" when a crazed fan tries to assassinate him. The Blonde is a beautiful young woman with a history of attempted suicides, about which she always has second thoughts; she calls for help before it's too late. This scene takes place at night, after Willy and the Blonde have gone to bed together. Although Willy was unable to perform sexually, she tells him not to worry about it—"I've had worse."

BLONDE: You're not like I thought you'd be. [. . .] See, I heard they were making a movie of your life story and all, and I thought you must be sorta adventurous for them to do that. And sorta dangerous. And sorta comical in all the witty things you must all the time sorta say. And like, if you have any influence and could set up an audition . . . *(Pause)* Movies are great, you know? Sometimes in movies everybody is sad? Somebody has died and everybody is in mourning. Everybody is miserable and they still seem to be having a better time than I ever have. On my best days even. I thought you'd be like that. Having a better time. [. . .]

    I don't know. You're nice but you seem . . . sad. *Sad*-sad. Don't be sad. At least you'll always be able to say you were famous for a little while. I'd give anything to be like you. Noticed. Most of us never get noticed for anything. I want more than that. I want . . . I want men to threaten to throw themselves off tall buildings if I won't marry them. And when I won't? They do. I'd like to feign humility while all the time accepting important awards. Thank you, everyone, thank you. I'd like to thank . . . me. I want . . . I want . . . I don't know what I want. It all.

14

"THE HAPPIEST MOMENT OF ALL?"

THREE TALL WOMEN

By Edward Albee

A wealthy, acerbic, aristocratic widow, A looks back on her life in Edward Albee's Pulitzer Prize–winning meditation on a woman's life. In this, the final speech of the play, A tells B and C, her younger selves, what life's happiest moment really was.

A *(Shakes her head; chuckles; to B and C)*: You're both such children. The happiest moment of all? Really? The happiest moment? *(To the audience now)* Coming to the end of it, I think, when all the waves cause the greatest woes subside, leaving breathing space, time to concentrate on the greatest woe of all—that blessed one—the end of it. Going through the whole thing and coming out . . . not out *beyond* it, of course, but sort of to . . . one side. None of that "further shore" nonsense, but to the point where you *can* think about yourself in the third person without being crazy. I've waked up in the morning, and I've thought, well, now, she's waking up, and now she's going to see what works—the eyes, for example. Can she *see*? She *can*? Well, good, I suppose; so much for that. Now she's going to test all the other stuff—the joints, the inside of the mouth, and now she's going to have to pee. What's she going to do—go for the walker. Lurch from chair to chair—pillar to post? Is she going to call for somebody— anybody . . . the tiniest thought there might be nobody there, that she's not making a sound, that maybe she's not alive—so's anybody'd notice, that is? *I* can do that. I can think about myself that way, which means, I suppose, that that's the way I'm *living*—beside myself, to one side. Is that what they mean by that? I'm beside myself? I don't think so. I think they're talking about *another* kind of joy. There's a difference between knowing you're going to *die* and *knowing* you're going to die. The second is better; it moves away from the theoretical. I'm rambling, aren't I?

[B *(Gently; face forward)*: A little.]

A *(To B)*: Well, we *do* that at ninety, or whatever I'm supposed to be; I mean, give a girl a break! *(To the audience again now)* Sometimes when I wake up and start thinking about myself like that—like I was watching—I really get the feeling that I *am dead*, but going on at the same time, and I wonder if she can talk and fear and . . . and then I wonder which has died—me, or the one I think about. It's a fairly confusing business. I'm rambling! *(A gestures to stop B)* Yes; I know! *(To the audience)* I was talking about . . . what: coming to the end of it; yes. So. There it is. You asked, after all. That's the happiest moment.

(A looks to C and B, puts her hand out, takes theirs.)

A: When it's all done. When we stop. When we can stop.

PTERODACTYLS

By Nicky Silver

In an introductory note, Nicky Silver calls this black comedy about a wealthy, supremely dysfunctional, American family "a play about, among other things, systems of denial and the price they carry in the world today." For Emma Duncan, twenty, the price is tragic. Her brother Todd has come home to be with his family after discovering he has AIDS, and ends up seducing Emma's fiancé Tommy. Emma's wedding dreams end—literally—with a bang on the day before the marriage, when she sees them embrace and shoots herself (the gun was a wedding present from Todd). In this speech, after her death, she talks directly to the audience.

EMMA: Hello everybody. I'm dead. How are you? I'm glad I killed myself. I'm not recommending it for others, mind you— no Dr. Kevorkian am I. But it's worked out for me. Looking back, I don't think I was ever supposed to have been born to begin with. Of course the idea that anything is "supposed to be" implies a master plan, and I don't believe in that kind of thing.

When I say I shouldn't have been born, I mean that my life was never all that pleasant. And there was no real reason for it. I was pretty. I had money. I was lucky enough to be born in a time and into a class where I had nothing but opportunities. I look around and there are crippled people and blind people and refugees and I can't believe I had the gall to whine about anything! I had my health—oh sure, I complained a lot, but really I was fine. And I had love! Granted the object of my affections was a latent, or not-so-latent homosexual as it turned out, who was infected with the HIV virus, who in turn infected me and my unborn baby—but isn't that really picking nits?

I can never thank Todd enough for giving me the gun, because for the first time, I'm happy. The pain is gone and I remember everything. Tommy is here, but we're not speaking. He spends all his time with Montgomery Clift and George Cukor talking about movies. I assume.

And I've been reunited with Alice Paulker. We went to school together. She was shot last year by a disgruntled postal worker. She has long, wavy brown hair and skin so pale you can see right through it—I don't mean it's really transparent and you can see her guts and organs and everything. It's just pale. And she has very big eyes, green. And we listen to music and go for walks. We take turns reading aloud to each other. She reads poems by Emily Brontë and I read chapters from *The Tropic of Cancer* by Henry Miller. She was always classier than me. And sometimes, we don't read. Sometimes, we just hold each other. And I run my fingers through her hair and she touches her lips, gently, along my cheek. She makes soft sounds, comforting sounds and she takes her time and she runs her tongue along the edge of my ear. We take off our clothes and just look at each other. I was shy at first, but Alice helped me and never rushed me. She held my breasts in her hands and ran her lips between them, down my stomach. I touch her eyelids and her forehead and her hair and her fingers and the back of her neck. And she enters me and I am everywhere at once and nowhere at all. And I remember everything and find that nothing matters. And for a moment, for a moment or two that lasts forever, we become one person. And I forget, we forget, that we were ever alive. And everything makes perfect sense.

BETTY'S SUMMER VACATION

By Christopher Durang

Betty's summer vacation did not turn out as she expected. Instead of a nice, quiet, restful stay at a summer cottage, Betty finds herself sharing her vacation home with, among others, a serial killer, an insane derelict and Three Voices who live in the ceiling. After a harrowing ordeal involving rape, murder, dismemberment and a mock COURT TV trial, Betty narrowly escapes death when the Voices allow her to flee the cottage moments before it blows up with everyone else inside.

This is the epilogue to the play; Betty is on the beach, in her nightgown, with the house burning behind her.

BETTY *(Speedy, upset, to herself)*: Where am I going to sleep tonight? I don't know why the people in the ceiling let me leave. I don't think I could have saved Mrs. Siezmagraff. I don't feel too guilty about it. I mean, they all seemed really terrible. I feel bad for Trudy, sort of . . . but well, I don't know what to think. *(Looks out, includes the audience in her thoughts now)* Now, actually, I think I'd like to become a hermit. Or I might become a nun if I could live in a convent in an isolated area with no other people around, and where no one in the convent is allowed to speak *ever*. I'd like that if it was quiet, and peaceful, and if they didn't care if I believed in God or not. *(Another idea)* Or maybe I could start my own community where people don't speak. And we'd plant our own food, and we'd watch the birds in the trees. And maybe I'm having a breakdown. *(Holds the sides of her head, as if it might fly apart)* Or is it a breakthrough? *(Hopeful; another possibility)* Maybe it's a bad dream I had, and am still having. *(Looks around her)* But I seem to be on the beach. And the house seems to be smoldering somewhere behind me in the distance. *(The sound of the ocean)* Isn't the sound of the ocean wonderful? *(Calming down slightly)* What is it about it that sounds so wonderful? But it does. It makes me feel good. It makes me feel connected. *(Realizing what she said before was a little off)* Well, maybe I don't have to join a convent where they don't speak. Maybe that's overreacting. But it is hard to be around civilization. I don't like people. But there are nice people, though, aren't there? Yes. I'm sure you're very nice—although I'm just trying to ingratiate myself to you so you don't try to cut any of my body parts off. *(Laughs, then cries)* Now I'm sad. *(Suddenly looks up, scared)* Now I'm frightened. *(The emotions pass)* No, now I'm fine. Listen to the ocean. That's why I wanted to come on this vacation, and have a summer share at the beach. I wanted to hear the ocean. But you know I forgot to listen to it the whole time I was with those people. But I'm going to listen to it now. *(She listens and with her we hear the sound of the waves; tension leaves Betty's face and body)* Oh, that's lovely. Yes. Ocean, waves, sand. I'm starting to feel better. *(Smiles. Closes her eyes. Continues to relax her body. The sound of the ocean continues . . .)*

MARISOL

By José Rivera

At the dawn of the millennium, New York is an apocalyptic battleground. Marisol's Guardian Angel has left her to lead the Heavenly Hierarchies in an insurrection against God. Their revolution has spilled down to Earth, where "time is crippled, geography's deformed" and derelicts and skinheads wield machine guns. At the end of the play, Marisol is killed in a round of bullets fired by a woman with an Uzi. All around her, however, are signs of triumph and hope, in this final speech of the play. Marisol stands alone, bathed in a spotlight.

MARISOL: I'm killed instantly. Little blazing lead meteors enter my body. My blood cells ride those bullets into outer space. My soul surges up the oceans of the Milky Way at the speed of light. At the moment of my death, I see the invisible war. Thousands of years of fighting pass in an instant. New and terrible forms of warfare, monstrous weapons, and unimagined strains of terror are created and destroyed in billionths of a second. Galaxies spring from a single drop of angel's sweat while hundreds of armies fight and die on the fingertips of children in the Bronx.

Three hundred million million beautiful rebel angels die in the first charge of the Final Battle. The oceans are salty with rebel blood. Angels drop like lightning from the collapsing sky. The angels are in full retreat. There's chaos. There's sorrow. There's blood and fire and ambulances and Heaven's soldiers scream and fight and die in beautiful, terrible light. It looks like the revolution is doomed.

Then, as if one body, one mind, the innocent of the earth take to the streets with anything they can find—rocks, sticks, fires—and aim their rage at the senile sky and fire into the tattered wind on the side of the rebels . . . billions of poor, of homeless, of peaceful, of silent, of angry . . . standing and screaming and fighting as no species has ever fought before. Inspired by the earthly noise, the rebels advance. New ideas rip the Heavens. New powers are created. New miracles are signed into Law. It's the first day of the new history.

Oh God. What light. What possibilities. What hope.

FURTHER READING

At *American Theatre* magazine/TCG we have been honored to work with the following writers to provide a permanent home for their art. We urge you to further explore the work of these exceptional artists.

This list is compiled alphabetically by author. The *American Theatre* issue information comes first; book publication information, if available, is set last.

EDWARD ALBEE
Three Tall Women, September 1994; published by Plume, a division of Penguin Putnam Inc., New York, 1995.

JON ROBIN BAITZ
Three Hotels, September 1993; from *Three Hotels: Plays and Monologues*, TCG, New York, 1994.

ERIC BOGOSIAN
Talk Radio, November 1987; from *The Essential Bogosian*, TCG, New York, 1994.

DON DELILLO
The Day Room, September 1986; published by Viking Press, a division of Penguin Putnam Inc., New York, 1989.

RITA DOVE

The Darker Face of the Earth, November 1996; published by Story Line Press, Ashland, OR, 3rd Edition, 2000.

CHRISTOPHER DURANG

Betty's Summer Vacation, December 1999; published by Grove/Atlantic, Inc., New York, 2000.

The Marriage of Bette and Boo, March 1986; published by Grove/Atlantic, Inc., New York, 1987.

ELIZABETH EGLOFF

The Swan, January 1992; published by Dramatists Play Service, Inc., New York, 1994.

DAVID FELDSHUH

Miss Evers' Boys, November 1990; published by Dramatists Play Service, Inc., New York, 1998.

MARIA IRENE FORNES

Abingdon Square, February 1988; published by Green Integer, Los Angeles, 2000.

JANUSZ GLOWACKI

Hunting Cockroaches, May 1987; from *Hunting Cockroaches and Other Plays*, Northwestern University Press, Evanstown, IL, 1990.

PHILIP KAN GOTANDA

Ballad of Yachiyo, February 1996; published by TCG, New York, 1997.

RICHARD GREENBERG

Three Days of Rain, March 1998; from *Three Days of Rain and Other Plays*, Grove/Atlantic, Inc., New York, 1999.

STUART GREENMAN
Silence, Cunning, Exile, January 1994.

KEVIN KLING
Lloyd's Prayer, November 1988.

HOWARD KORDER
Search and Destroy, June 1990; published by Grove/Atlantic, Inc., New York, 1992.

TONY KUSHNER
Angels in America, Part One: Millennium Approaches, June 1992; published by TCG, New York, 1992, 1993, 1995.

CHRISTOPHER KYLE
The Monogamist, March 1996; published by Dramatists Play Service, Inc., New York, 1996.

DAVID LINDSAY-ABAIRE
Fuddy Meers, July 2000; published by Overlook Press, New York, 2001.

LISA LOOMER
The Waiting Room, December 1994; published by Dramatists Play Service, Inc., New York, 1998.

CRAIG LUCAS
Reckless, January 1989; from *Reckless and Other Plays*, TCG, New York, 2003.

DAVID MAMET
Three Sisters (adapted from the play by Anton Chekhov), July 1991; published by Grove/Atlantic, Inc., New York, 1991.

STEVE MARTIN
Picasso at the Lapin Agile, November 1994; from *Picasso at the Lapin Agile and Other Plays*, Grove/Atlantic, Inc., New York, 1997.

ELLEN MCLAUGHIN
Tongue of a Bird, March 1999; published by Samuel French, Inc., New York, 2000.

SCOTT MCPHERSON
Marvin's Room, March 1992; published by Penguin Putnam, Inc., New York, 1992.

CHARLES L. MEE
bobrauschenbergamerica, September 2001; available at www. charlesmee.org.

STEPHEN METCALFE
The Incredibly Famous Willy Rivers, January 1986.

MARLANE MEYER
The Chemistry of Change, September 1998.

DAEL ORLANDERSMITH
The Gimmick, September 1999; from *Beauty's Daughter, Monster, The Gimmick: Three Plays*, Vintage Books, a division of Random House, Inc., New York, 2000.

SUZAN-LORI PARKS
In the Blood, March 2000; from *The Red Letter Plays*, TCG, New York, 2001.

REYNOLDS PRICE
August Snow, January 1990; from *New Music*, TCG, New York, 1990.

DAVID RABE
A Question of Mercy, July 1997; published by Grove/Atlantic, Inc., New York, 1998.

JOSÉ RIVERA

Marisol, July 1993; from *Marisol and Other Plays*, TCG, New York, 1997.

MILCHA SANCHEZ-SCOTT

Roosters, September 1987; published by Dramatists Play Service, Inc., New York, 1998.

SAM SHEPARD

Buried Child, September 1996; from *Sam Shepard: Seven Plays*, Bantam Doubleday Dell, a division of Random House, Inc., New York, 1984.

NICKY SILVER

Pterodactyls, February 1994; from *Etiquette and Vitriol: The Food Chain and Other Plays*, TCG, New York, 1996.

DIANA SON

Stop Kiss, July 1999; published by Overlook Press, New York, 2000.

PAULA VOGEL

The Mineola Twins, February 1997; from *The Mammary Plays*, TCG, New York, 1998.

WENDY WASSERSTEIN

An American Daughter, September 1997; published by Harvest Books, a division of Harcourt, Inc., New York, 1999.

GEORGE C. WOLFE

The Colored Museum, February 1987; published by Grove/Atlantic, Inc., New York, 1988.

The following list provides contact information regarding performance rights to the works included in this volume:

Edward Albee c/o William Morris Agency, 1325 Ave. of the Americas, NY, NY 10019; Jon Robin Baitz c/o Creative Artists Agency, 767 Fifth Ave., NY, NY 10153; Eric Bogosian c/o Creative Artists Agency, 767 Fifth Ave., NY, NY 10153; Don DeLillo c/o The Wallace Agency, 177 E. 70th St., NY, NY 10021; Rita Dove c/o Story Line Press, Three Oaks Farm, Box 1240, Ashland, OR 97520-0055; Christopher Durang c/o Helen Merrill, Ltd., 295 Lafayette St., Suite 915, NY, NY 10012; Elizabeth Egloff c/o International Creative Management, 40 W. 57th St., NY, NY 10019; David Feldshuh c/o Helen Merrill, Ltd., 295 Lafayette St., Suite 915, NY, NY 10012; Maria Irene Fornes c/o Helen Merrill Ltd., 295 Lafayette St., Suite 915, NY, NY 10012; Janusz Glowacki c/o International Creative Management, 40 W. 57th St., NY, NY 10019; Philip Kan Gotanda c/o Helen Merrill, Ltd., 295 Lafayette St., Suite 915, NY, NY 10012; Richard Greenberg c/o Creative Artists Agency, 767 Fifth Ave., NY, NY 10153; Stuart Greenman c/o TCG; Kevin Kling c/o Susan Schulman, A Literary Agency, 454 W. 44th St., NY, NY 10036; Howard Korder c/o Abrams Artists Agency, 275 Seventh Ave., 26th Floor, NY, NY 10001; Tony Kushner c/o Joyce Ketay Agency, 630 Ninth Ave., Suite 706, NY, NY 10036; Christopher Kyle c/o Schreck Rose & Dapello, 660 Madison Ave., 10th Floor, NY, NY 10021; David Lindsay-Abaire c/o The Gersh Agency, 41 Madison Ave., NY, NY 10010; Lisa Loomer c/o The Gersh Agency, 41 Madison Ave., NY, NY 10010; Craig Lucas c/o The Gersh

Agency, 41 Madison Ave., NY, NY 10010; David Mamet c/o Rosenstone/Wender, 38 E. 29th St., 10th Floor, NY, NY 10016; Steve Martin c/o International Creative Management, 40 W. 57th St., NY, NY 10019; Ellen McLaughlin c/o Joyce Ketay Agency, 630 Ninth Ave., Suite 706, NY, NY 10036; Scott McPherson c/o Scout Productions, Inc., 53 W. Jackson Blvd., Suite 1534, Chicago, IL 60604; Charles L. Mee c/o International Creative Management, 40 W. 57th St., NY, NY 10019; Stephen Metcalfe c/o TCG; Marlane Meyer c/o The Gersh Agency, 41 Madison Ave., NY, NY 10010; Dael Orlandersmith c/o Berman, Boals and Flynn, 208 W. 30th St., Suite 401, NY, NY 10001; Suzan-Lori Parks c/o Creative Artists Agency, 767 Fifth Ave., NY, NY 10153; Reynolds Price c/o William Morris Agency, 1325 Ave. of the Americas, NY, NY 10019; David Rabe c/o Joyce Ketay Agency, 630 Ninth Ave., Suite 706, NY, NY 10036; José Rivera c/o Joyce Ketay Agency, 630 Ninth Ave., Suite 706, NY, NY 10036; Milcha Sanchez-Scott c/o William Morris Agency, 1325 Ave. of the Americas, NY, NY 10019; Sam Shepard c/o Berman, Boals and Flynn, 208 W. 30th St., Suite 401, NY, NY 10001; Nicky Silver c/o Creative Artists Agency, 767 Fifth Ave., NY, NY 10153; Diana Son c/o International Creative Management, 40 W. 57th St., NY, NY 10019; Paula Vogel c/o The Gersh Agency, 41 Madison Ave., NY, NY 10010; Wendy Wasserstein c/o Rosenstone/Wender, 38 E. 29th St., 10th Floor, NY, NY 10016; George C. Wolfe c/o Loeb & Loeb, 345 Park Ave., 18th Floor, NY, NY 10154.

STEPHANIE COEN is the director of communications at Seattle's Intiman Theatre. Previously, she was director of publications for The Joseph Papp Public Theater/New York Shakespeare Festival under the artistic leadership of George C. Wolfe. A former managing editor of *American Theatre* magazine, she was on staff at Theatre Communications Group for seven years and wrote TCG's 2000 report on the state of the American theatre, "The Field and Its Challenges."